WordPress Plugin Development
Beginner's Guide

006.7

Build powerful, interactive plugins for your blog and to share online

Vladimir Prelovac

PUBLISHING

BIRMINGHAM - MUMBAI

WordPress Plugin Development

Beginner's Guide

First published: February 2009

Production Reference: 2200209

Published by Packt Publishing Ltd.
32 Lincoln Road
Olton
Birmingham, B27 6PA, UK.

ISBN 978-1-847193-59-9

www.packtpub.com

Cover Image by Vinayak Chittar (vinayak.chittar@gmail.com)

Credits

Author

Vladimir Prelovac

Reviewer

Junal Rahman

Senior Acquisition Editor

David Barnes

Development Editor

Nikhil Bangera

Technical Editor

Mehul Shetty

Copy Editor

Sumathi Sridhar

Indexer

Monica Ajmera

Production Editorial Manager

Abhijeet Deobhakta

Editorial Team Leader

Akshara Aware

Project Team Leader

Lata Basantani

Project Coordinator

Neelkanth Mehta

Proofreader

Lesley Harrison

Production Coordinator

Shantanu Zagade

Cover Work

Shantanu Zagade

About the Author

Vladimir Prelovac is the author of many popular WordPress plugins and articles about WordPress optimization, security and maintenance. He actively uses WordPress platform as a base for Internet development strategy for small & mid-sized businesses.

For Vladimir, WordPress development is a full time job about which he happily blogs on his web site www.prelovac.com/vladimir.

I'd like to thank my editor Mr. Barnes, for leading me through the book writer's path. Dave, Ervin, and guys at Wordcast, for the professional support they showed in such a lovely way. My family for understanding the long, sleepless nights of writing. Finally, I wish to dedicate this book to my mother, Vera Prelovac (1949-2008), who was and will always be my beacon of light.

About the Reviewer

Junal Rahman is a Computer Science graduate from the Independent University of Bangladesh. His areas of expertise include programming with the PHP framework and creating Facebook applications. He has worked for several software companies as a Web Application Developer. During his undergraduate studies Junal fell in love with .NET programming, but as soon as he started his internship, he fell in love with PHP. He currently works as a Development Engineer at Trippert Labs. At Trippert, Junal collaboratively works to create Facebook applications. He also maintains a blog that can be found at `http://junal.wordpress.com`.

I would like to acknowledge my sister Shiuly, follow your dreams

Table of Contents

Preface

If you can write WordPress plugins, you can make WordPress do just about anything. From making the site easier to administer, to adding the odd tweak or new feature, to completely changing the way your blog works; plugins are the method WordPress offers to customize and extend its functionality. This book will show you how to build all sorts of WordPress plugins: admin plugins, Widgets, plugins that alter your post output, present custom "views" of your blog, and more.

This book focuses on teaching you all aspects of modern WordPress development and usage. The book uses real and published WordPress plugins and follows their creation from the idea to the finishing touches, in a series of carefully picked, easy-to-follow tutorials. You will discover how to use the WordPress API in all typical situations, from displaying output on the site in the beginning to turning WordPress into a CMS in the last chapter. In Chapters 2 to 7, you will develop six concrete plugins and conquer all aspects of WordPress plugin development.

Each new chapter and each new plugin introduces different features of WordPress and how to put them to good use, allowing you to gradually advance your knowledge. This book is written as a guide to take your WordPress skills from the very beginning to the level where you are able to completely understand how WordPress works and how you can use it to your advantage.

This is a Packt Beginners Guide, which means it focuses on practical examples and has a fast-paced but friendly approach, with the opportunity to learn by experimentation and play. Each chapter builds a practical plugin from the ground up using step-by-step instructions. Individual sections show you how to code some functionality into your plugin and follow up with a discussion of concepts.

What This Book Covers

Chapter 1 teaches the advantages of WordPress development, and what WordPress has to offer to plugin authors.

Chapter 2 creates a working, useful, and attractive WordPress plugin from scratch. It shows how to extract information using the WordPress API and how to use CSS to improve the look of our plugin.

Chapter 3 explores more cool things we can do with WordPress by livening up the default WordPress blogroll. The purpose of the plugin is to display the most recent posts from the sites listed in the blogroll using a nice pop-up window.

Chapter 4 uses the mixed approach, by taking advantage of creative WordPress and JavaScript techniques, in order to create an Ajax powered 'Wall' for your blog's sidebar. It introduces quite a few interesting techniques such as Widgets, interacting with the WordPress Database, and Ajax form submission.

Chapter 5 covers the creation of a very sleek and stylish looking WordPress enhancement. The purpose of the Snazzy Archives plugin will be to present your site archives in a unique visual way. It shows how to manipulate the layout of the template using shortcodes and custom templates.

Chapter 6 is all about digging a little deeper into WordPress and hacking the Write Post screen. It shows how to create custom panels in the various sections of the Write Post screen. It teaches how to access the current WordPress rich text editor, tinyMCE, and create a button on its toolbar.

Chapter 7 explores the possibilities of turning WordPress into a Content Management System (CMS), using methods provided to us by WordPress. It shows how to modify the Manage Posts panel to display the information we want. It also covers managing who can use your plugin by looking at the logged in user capabilities.

Chapter 8 covers the additional steps involved in localizing, documenting, publishing, and promoting your plugin. It also covers useful tips and ideas to improve your general WordPress knowledge further.

Who is This Book For

This book is for programmers working with WordPress, who want to develop custom plugins and to hack the code base. You need to be familiar with the basics of WordPress and PHP programming and believe that code is poetry; this book will handle the rest.

Conventions

In this book, you will find a number of styles of text that distinguish between different kinds of information. Here are some examples of these styles, and an explanation of their meaning.

Code words in text are shown as follows: "Edit the insights.js file and add the functionality to insert the HTML directly into tinyMCE."

A block of code will be set as follows:

```
/* Add Digg link to the end of the post */
function WPDiggThis_ContentFilter($content)
{
        return $content.WPDiggThis_Link();
}
```

When we wish to draw your attention to a particular part of a code block, the relevant lines or items will be made bold:

```
<?php the_content('<p class="serif">Read the rest of this entry
&raquo;</p>'); ?>

<?php if (function_exists(WPDiggThis_Link)) echo WPDiggThis_Link(); ?>
```

New terms and **important words** are introduced in a bold-type font. Words that you see on the screen, in menus or dialog boxes for example, appear in our text like this:

"Go to your WordPress **Plugins** admin panel."

 Warnings or important notes appear in a box like this.

 Tips and tricks appear like this.

Reader Feedback

Feedback from our readers is always welcome. Let us know what you think about this book, what you liked or may have disliked. Reader feedback is important for us to develop titles that you really get the most out of.

To send us general feedback, simply drop an email to feedback@packtpub.com, making sure to mention the book title in the subject of your message.

If there is a book that you need and would like to see us publish, please send us a note in the **SUGGEST A TITLE** form on www.packtpub.com or email suggest@packtpub.com.

If there is a topic that you have expertise in and you are interested in either writing or contributing to a book, see our author guide on www.packtpub.com/authors.

Customer Support

Now that you are the proud owner of a Packt book, we have a number of things to help you to get the most from your purchase.

Downloading the Example Code for the Book

Visit http://www.packtpub.com/files/code/3599_Code.zip to directly download the example code.

The downloadable files contain instructions on how to use them.

Errata

Although we have taken every care to ensure the accuracy of our contents, mistakes do happen. If you find a mistake in one of our books—maybe a mistake in text or code—we would be grateful if you would report this to us. By doing this you can save other readers from frustration, and help to improve subsequent versions of this book. If you find any errata, report them by visiting http://www.packtpub.com/support, selecting your book, clicking on the **let us know** link, and entering the details of your errata. Once your errata are verified, your submission will be accepted and the errata are added to the list of existing errata. The existing errata can be viewed by selecting your title from http://www.packtpub.com/support.

Piracy

Piracy of copyright material on the Internet is an ongoing problem across all media. At Packt, we take the protection of our copyright and licenses very seriously. If you come across any illegal copies of our works in any form on the Internet, please provide the location address or website name immediately so we can pursue a remedy.

Please contact us at `copyright@packtpub.com` with a link to the suspected pirated material.

We appreciate your help in protecting our authors, and our ability to bring you valuable content.

Questions

You can contact us at `questions@packtpub.com` if you are having a problem with some aspect of the book, and we will do our best to address it.

1

Preparing for WordPress Development

If you are holding this book in your hands now, you are probably aware—in one way or the other—of the tremendous success WordPress platform has seen over the past few years. It has become the most widespread blogging and publishing platform in the world today.

When I first installed WordPress, I was still looking around for a platform to start my personal site and also for an opportunity to do more online development work.

After seeing the simple installation procedure (which takes just a few minutes), I realized that the guys behind WordPress are on to something big. It has indeed proven to be so, and as the days passed by, I have enjoyed every aspect of WordPress—publishing, social, and development.

And I am thrilled to share these nits and bits of WordPress development information with you, showing you the power and flexibility that allowed WordPress to become so popular.

How will you benefit?

Thanks to its open source architecture, ease of use, and customization possibilities, WordPress has succeeded in differentiating itself from other weblog publishing platforms and even other open source solutions.

WordPress features

The main WordPress features of interest to developers are:

- Its a huge community of users and developers
- The millions of WordPress blogs
- Major sites using it, including a number of US government agencies

- ◆ Security issues treated almost instantly
- ◆ Unmatched flexibility with thousands of available plugins
- ◆ High level of customizability with thousands of available themes
- ◆ Search engine friendly functionalities
- ◆ Ease of use, maintenance, and upgrade
- ◆ A great way to meet new people!

With such a list, it is no wonder that—every day—more and more private users and companies are turning to WordPress for their publishing needs. This of course presents a fertile ground for WordPress developers to show off their skills.

More sites means more opportunities

The opportunity for a WordPress developer in these circumstances becomes obvious.

With such a huge number of sites running it, the market is **hungry** for WordPress experts, and not just development experts. If you are proficient in the installation and setup of WordPress, you may easily have your hands full of work.

Big players use it

The fact that a number of major sites use WordPress means that there is also an opportunity for **high profile** work.

This also means that you can be fairly certain about the future of WordPress. Your investment in time and efforts, first in reading this book, and then in enhancing your development skills, is likely to pay off with WordPress.

Urgent response to security issues

With online security becoming a bigger issue each day, it is a relief to see the WordPress development team reacting promptly to newly discovered security issues.

This makes everyone even more comfortable and confident in using WordPress.

Flexibility

With WordPress, the plugin author is allowed total control over every aspect of the site. You are able to completely customize the way the site looks and behaves.

The opportunity is there for everyone—from beginners (developing useful plugins) to professionals (creating total WordPress makeovers such as e-commerce, marketing, or job portal sites—where you can hardly recognize that the site is running a WordPress installation).

Search engines friendly

Search Engine Optimization (SEO) is an important aspect of today's Internet presence. Just creating a site is not enough anymore, as there are now hundreds of millions of competing websites out there.

Using a platform such as WordPress will be really valuable, especially in the long term. WordPress has significant built-in SEO features and also most of the other aspects of modern SEO technologies available through custom plugins (and you can always write one to match your needs!)

 Becoming proficient in SEO concepts can help you a lot as a WordPress developer, as the need for both WordPress and SEO skills is growing fast.

Easy to use

WordPress is meant for beginners and used by professionals. This mix is rarely seen in any other open source platforms.

After the five minute installation, most users immediately feel comfortable in the WordPress administration panels. Writing a post and organizing categories is as simple as it should be.

The whole WordPress installation consists of putting the files on the server and setting the assigned database, and it is very easy to back up or move it to another server.

WordPress and its plugins can be upgraded with a click of a button; all this makes the job of maintaining a WordPress website (or even several at the same time), a breeze.

Social aspect

If you are a WordPress developer, the chances are that you will have your own hosted WordPress blog. Having a personal blog creates a great opportunity to create many new contacts—both business and friends.

When you release a WordPress plugin, you will meet hundreds of people who are going to use it on their own sites. You will also have people visit you for support, or just to say **Thank you**!

Plugins as tool for promotion

With such a huge user base, a well written plugin will probably be downloaded tens of thousands of times.

This will create awareness about you as a plugin author and your site as a probable source for some **cool** stuff. Having in mind how difficult it is to get noticed on the Internet today, this becomes a very important aspect of plugin development that you get **for free**.

Creating fresh, new, and usable plugins can help you go a long way. It has really helped me a lot in my field of work and has created a lot of opportunities–one certainly being, the pleasure of writing this book.

Dogfooding WordPress plugins

You may sometimes wish to create a plugin just for yourself, to fulfil a specific need that can arise at a given moment. This is how I started writing plugins initially, as I needed certain functionalities that were not available in WordPress at the time.

The term **dogfooding** describes a dog food company that is ready to **eat its own dog food**. It means the company is confident about its own product and uses it for the purpose it was produced for.

In WordPress' terms, it means that you should always strive to create a plugin that satisfies your needs. On my personal site, I still use almost all of the plugins I created, and I only update them over time, as and when WordPress is updated, or my needs change.

This has a positive side effect of ensuring that your plugins will probably be attractive to many other users as well. Assuming that you are critical about your own work, and your confidence in using your own plugins sends out a clear message on how good they are.

Challenges involved

Developing WordPress plugins is not always an easy job. It brings a number of challenges that you will need to overcome.

Development

WordPress uses PHP and provides an API with its own functions. The API has grown over time, and now covers all possible methods of communication between WordPress and the plugin.

This book will cover all the aspects of the API with practical examples, and the development of six concrete plugins (chapters 2-7). Through step-by-step guides to creating these plugins, you will discover how to use API in typical situations, from displaying output on the site in the beginning, to turning WordPress into a CMS at the end.

Each new chapter and each new plugin will introduce different features of WordPress, and how to put them to good use, thereby allowing you to gradually advance your knowledge.

Security

As much as WordPress team takes care of the WordPress core, you need to take care of security in your plugins. Always remember that your plugin is given the ultimate authority on the user's site. This is a great feature that allowed WordPress to become popular; but with that it also carries a great deal of responsibility.

This book will show the methods and functions best suited to the given situations, and underline the security implications. There are not too many issues to worry about, so make sure you remember the implications and best practices and apply them to your plugins.

Work after development

Once the development work is done and the plugin is finished, a lot of authors face the question: What now? If you plan to release the plugin to the public, there are a few extra steps you need to take care of.

This book will give you practical tips in this area—refer to Chapter 8.

It will cover the process that takes you from the end of the development phase to the first users coming back to you with feedback and questions. I have learned much from my own plugin development experience, and I will also be referencing some of the resources available online .

Localization

At the moment, WordPress is translated into more than 50 languages worldwide. The number of users using WordPress in their native language is growing each day, and they usually prefer using plugins that support their own language.

Localization in WordPress is easy, and the best thing is that you will not have to do any translation. There will always be users interested in translating your plugin to their own language and sending you the file back. This is the way it works, and it is mutually beneficial.

Documentation

Writing documentation is often boring work but I will show you templates which will help you to do it more efficiently and also point out the benefits of writing good documentation.

I will also cover the necessary steps to manage your plugin using **SVN (Subversion)**, and submit it to the WordPress Plugin Repository—the central repository of all WordPress plugins which currently hosts thousands of plugins and has served millions of downloads.

Support

Good documentation goes a long way when it comes to support.

You can expect hundreds of user questions pouring in after you release a plugin. So, making sure that you have a well written documentation will save you a lot of time in answering those questions.

I will also give some practical tips on how to organize your plugin page.

Promotion

Writing a good plugin that nobody knows about is a fruitless effort.

I will give you tips on how to promote your plugin once it is published. If you have created a really useful plugin, you can expect a snowball effect when users start to write about it on their blogs and tell their friends about it.

Plugins developed in this book

This introduction chapter is followed by seven chapters; six of which describe the creation of WordPress plugins and a final chapter dealing with post-development issues:

- Digg This
- Live Blogroll
- The Wall
- Snazzy Archives
- Insights
- Post Types
- Development Goodies

Various development topics and WordPress specific functions are introduced throughout the development of these plugins, using concrete, step-by-step practical examples.

Digg This

New WordPress plugin WP Digg This

The cool new WordPress plugin allows the user to easily add the Digg This functionality to their blog.

This post is used to test the functionality of the plugin.

This is the first plugin we will be developing. This plugin will show a Digg button in your blog posts.

The purpose of this plugin will also be to introduce you to the basic concepts of WordPress plugin development.

We will access some of the basic WordPress API functions, and talk about filters and actions which are the WordPress mechanisms for controlling the workflow of the site.

Live Blogroll

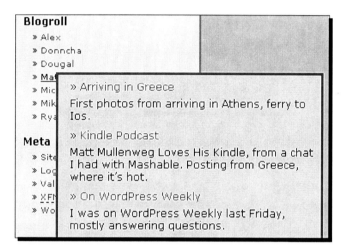

The second plugin comes from the idea of making the default blogroll look a little bit more exciting.

We will expand our knowledge of WordPress API, but also introduce two very important **allies** in WordPress plugin development, namely **jQuery** and **Ajax**.

jQuery and Ajax technologies help our plugins become more engaging, and we will learn the basic concepts of using them through a series of practical examples.

The Wall

Wall

admin: Thanks Dave!

guest: Hi there!

Nick: I wonder what the next plugin will be?

Dave: This Wall is looking good! I am going to use it on my blog.

Jedi: Have you watched Star Wars recently ?

Name

[   ]

Comment

[   ]

This chapter is all about WP Wall; a plugin that creates a shoutbox on your blog's sidebar, where users can leave **comments** and **shouts**.

The chapter teaches important lessons, including how to create a widget and interact with the WordPress database. It also expands the usage of Ajax to include dynamic interaction with the user.

I will also try to engage you to think about WordPress plugin development in a slightly different way.

Snazzy Archives

If plugins can be classified by beauty, this would be the most beautiful plugin in the book. It will display your blog archives in a way you probably have not seen before.

During the creation of the plugin, we will explore how to interact with posts, create plugin options, and manage them through a settings page in the administration. We will then use all that knowledge to produce a beautiful representation of your blog's archives.

Insights

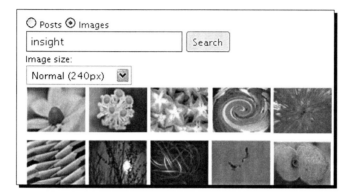

Insights plugin will add to the productivity of the blog owner by offering **quick access to common** information in the **Write Post** screen.

In this chapter, we will learn how to change the WordPress **Write Post** screen and interact with the built-in TinyMCE editor. We will use Ajax to get information delivered directly into our post while we write it!

Post Types

The final plugin of the book will see us working more closely with the WordPress backend, and explore ways to transform WordPress into a versatile **Content Management System (CMS)**.

We will learn how to customize the administration menus and pages, use custom fields to store additional information, explore user capabilities system, and use localization.

Development Goodies

After all the hard work in developing those plugins, comes a chapter dedicated to all the post-development work (after-hour party!).

The purpose of this chapter will be to explain localization, documentation, code management, and plugin promotion. It will also give you some information regarding **WordPress MU** development. Wordpress MU is a multi user version of WordPress that is becoming more popular each day.

Tools for the job

Before we get started, we need to have some tools set up, so let's go through a short check list.

Whatever way you decide to set up your development environment, make sure you are comfortable using it. Plugin development can be a full-time job, so make sure you enjoy it as much as you can!

WordPress

Obviously, we will need WordPress installed. It is advisable to have a separate version of WordPress for development purposes (that is, do not use your blog as a testing ground; your visitors will not like it very much).

To prepare your local version, you can always download the latest version of WordPress from `http://wordpress.org/download/`.

Then you need to decide if you are going to host it on the Internet or locally. I prefer to have it on Internet as I can easily show it to other people if necessary, no matter where I am at that moment. The advantage of local installation is that it works much faster. You can of course combine both.

If you are going to set it up on your local computer, and you are using Windows, using packages such as EasyPHP (`http://www.easyphp.org`) will make your job much easier. This is a software package that incorporates PHP and MySQL for Windows systems, and is free to use.

Installing WordPress is a simple matter. I recommend going to `http://codex.wordpress.org/Installing_WordPress` for the latest guide to the installation process.

If you would like to set up the latest development version, I suggest you read the section *Using SVN* in *Chapter 8*.

Text editor

Obviously, you are going to need a text editor. Any editor will do, and you probably have a preference by now.

You do not need your text editor to do anything fancy. Indentation support and syntax highlighting for PHP, HTML and JavaScript is almost all you need from an editor at this point.

I have been using UltraEdit for years, and it has been always my weapon of choice for a quick, small, and powerful editor. There also are other text editors that are available for free, such as, Netbeans IDE for PHP, Zend Studio, and so on.

FTP client

The second thing you will need to have is an FTP client. Uploading plugins can be a boring job if you do it from the FTP command line; so visual FTP client is advisable.

For this matter, I've been using Total Commander as a proven tool. Again, you might have your own preference.

Web browser

Finally, since we are developing web based software, we will need a web browser. You will be spending a lot of time in the browser window; so make sure you are comfortable with it.

I do not want to instigate browser wars at this moment, but there is one browser that is very flexible and has tons of add-ons, much like WordPress in that respect, and that is Firefox.

There are some pretty cool add-ons for Firefox that can really increase productivity to the level of rapid web development. This step is optional if you do not use Firefox, but I would nevertheless recommend giving it a try.

Firebug

The most important Firefox add-on we want to install is called Firebug (you can download it from `http://getfirebug.com`).

Firebug allows you to preview, edit and debug CSS, HTML, JavaScript and Ajax requests in real time. This is really a great time saver. For example, when it comes to debugging, JavaScript or misaligned CSS can be really troublesome, without the use of features provided by Firebug.

In the next picture, you can see an example of Firebug in action, debugging JavaScript with a breakpoint in the execution of the script.

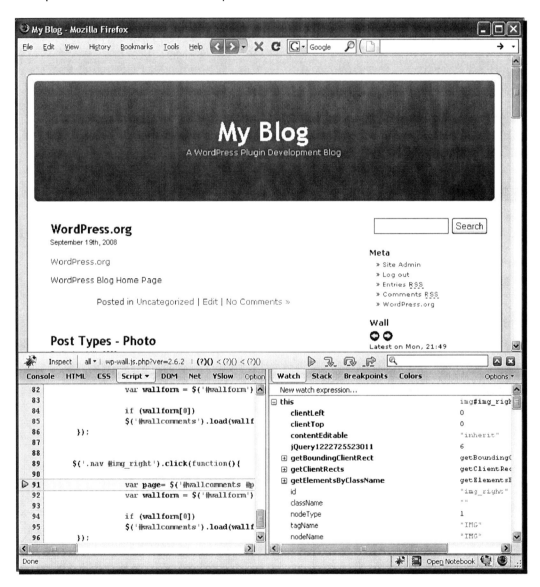

Ubiquity

This is an add-on produced by Mozilla Labs and it can do a lot of fancy stuff. But for our purposes, we are going to use it for two simple things—fast search of PHP and WordPress documentation.

You will need to install Ubiquity from `https://wiki.mozilla.org/Labs/Ubiquity` and also install these two plugins:

1. PHP Search: `http://npattison.com/ubiquity/ubiq_php.html`
2. WP Codex Search: `http://www.prelovac.com/vladimir/ubiquity-plugins/wp-codex-search`

The way these two Ubiquity commands work is that when you press *Ctrl* and *Space* in the browser (this opens Ubiquity window) and then type `php search_phrase` or `wp search_phrase`, it takes you immediately to the PHP or WordPress documentation for the given phrase.

The amount of time this can save is huge, especially if you need to take a peek at the documentation every minute or so like I do (I can't keep everything in my head!).

Screengrab

You can grab **Screengrab** from `http://www.screengrab.org`, and this plugin allows you to take screenshots from your browser window easily. It can capture an entire page, a visible portion, or a user selection on the page.

Once you get used it, you will use it extensively for creating images for your plugin documentation. I have used it for almost all the images in this book.

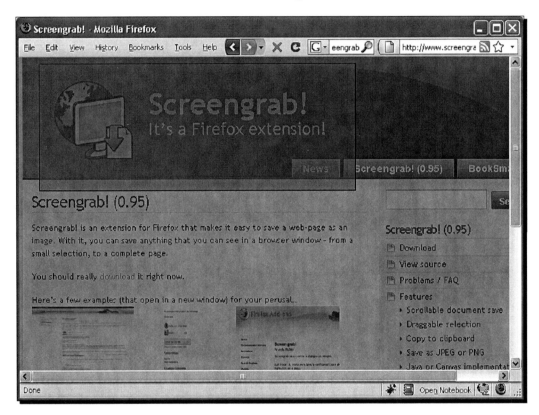

IE tab

This Firefox add-on allows you to quickly change the rendering engine between Firefox and the installed version of the Internet Explorer. It allows you to quickly check if your plugin behaves well in this browser.

You can get it from `http://ietab.mozdev.org/`.

Quick reference

WordPress: `http://www.wordpress.org/download`

Installing WordPress: `http://codex.wordpress.org/Installing_WordPress`

EasyPHP: `http://www.easyphp.org`

UltraEdit: `http://www.ultraedit.com`

Total Commander: `http://www.ghisler.com`

FireFox: `http://getfirefox.com`

FireBug: `http://getfirebug.com`

Ubiquity: `https://wiki.mozilla.org/Labs/Ubiquity`

PHP Search for Ubiquity: `http://npattison.com/ubiquity/ubiq_php.html`

WP Codex Search for Ubiquity: `http://www.prelovac.com/vladimir/ubiquity-plugins/wp-codex-search`

ScreenGrab: `http://www.screengrab.org`

IETab: `http://ietab.mozdev.org/`

Final notes

Before we start with development, let's have a quick reminder on how to install and manage WordPress plugins. Also I'll mention a handy tip for quickly accessing code examples.

Installing and managing plugins

When you want to install a plugin, you need to follow these simple steps:

1. Upload the plugin folder (for example `wp-wall`) to your server's `wp-content/plugins/` folder.

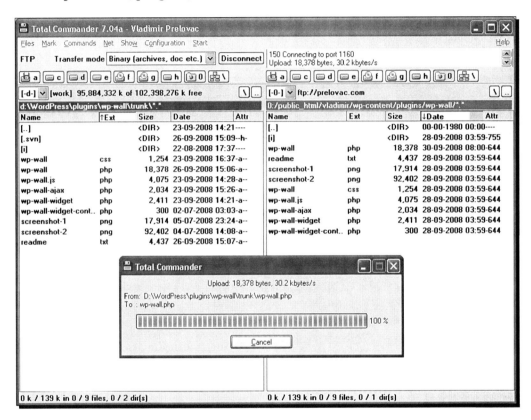

2. Go to your WordPress administration section, and select **Plugins** from the menu. This will give you a list of all the installed plugins. Scroll down the list until you find yours, and click **Activate**.

If you intend to manually update the plugin files on a live site, it is advisable to deactivate the plugin first using the Plugins menu.

Strictly speaking, on a development blog where you are the only user, this can be skipped to save time.

 If something goes wrong with the plugin, and you are unable to access your WordPress site anymore, deleting the plugin folder from the server will deactivate the plugin automatically, and will instantly get your site working again.

If you need more information regarding plugin management, you can refer to the latest WordPress manual found at `http://codex.wordpress.org/Managing_Plugins`.

Searching documentation

During the plugin development, you will more or less need to refer to documentation.

Luckily, you will have this book on your hand either in paper or in a PDF form, so you can take a quick look. Then, you also have the WordPress online documentation found at `http://codex.wordpress.org/Main_Page`.

Due to the rapid speed at which WordPress has been developing, not all the functions have been documented.

So, I keep a copy of the latest version of WordPress locally. This way, I am able to find the reference to the function in the WordPress core quickly, and figure out how it is used.

I also tend to keep a local copy of the entire plugin repository on my computer (you can find more details on how to do that in Chapter 8) so that I can search through the entire plugin repository and find instances of this function used by other plugin authors (and you can always find new and creative uses as well).

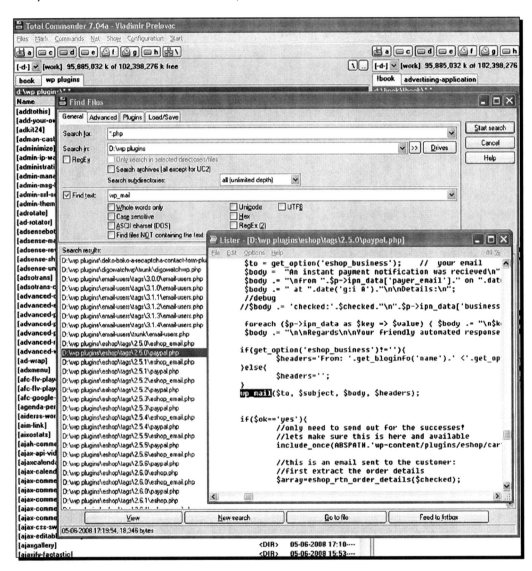

Using other plugins for this purpose can really save a lot of time, and it is often the easiest way to learn how to perform certain functionalities.

Summary

We learned about the advantages of WordPress development, and what WordPress has to offer to plugin authors. We have also seen that there are certain challenges along the way, which we will address in this book.

The six plugins that we will create in the following chapters will show you exactly how to create a WordPress plugin from scratch and have it perform the concrete functionality you need, whether it's on the front page or in the administration backend.

Having armed ourselves with useful development tools, we are ready to start developing some cool WordPress plugins!

2
Social Bookmarking

I hope the first chapter got you warmed up and prepared for WordPress plugin development, and that you are as eager to start as I am.

In this chapter, we will create our first functional WordPress plugin and learn how to interact with the WordPress API (this is the WordPress interface to PHP) on the way. The knowledge you will gain in this chapter alone will allow you to write a lot of similar plugins.

Let's get moving! In this chapter, you will learn:

- **Creating a new plugin** and having it displayed in the plugins admin panel
- Checking the **WordPress version** and **control activation** of the plugin
- **Accessing API features**—for example the title and permalink URL of each post
- Using **WordPress hooks** to execute your plugin code when it's needed
- Using **conditional tags** to control the flow of your plugins

You will learn these by:

- Creating a 'social bookmarking' type of plugin that adds a **Digg** button to each post on your blog

As you probably know, Digg is a very popular service for promoting interesting content on the Internet. The purpose of a **Digg** button on your blog is to make it easier for Digg users to vote for your article and also to bring in more visitors to your blog.

The plugin we'll create in this chapter will automatically insert the necessary code to each of your posts. So let's get started with WordPress plugin development!

Plugging in your first plugin

Usually, the first step in plugin creation is coming up with a plugin name. We usually want to use a name that is associated with what the plugin does, so we will call this plugin, **WP Digg This**. WP is a common prefix used to name WordPress plugins.

To introduce the plugin to WordPress, we need to create a standard plugin header. This will always be the first piece of code in the plugin file and it is used to identify the plugin to WordPress.

Time for action – Create your first plugin

In this example, we're going to write the code to register the plugin with WordPress , describe what the plugin does for the user, check whether it works on the currently installed version of WordPress, and to activate it.

1. Create a file called `wp-digg-this.php` in your favourite text editor. It is common practice to use the plugin name as the name for the plugin file, with dashes '-' instead of spaces.

2. Next, add a plugin information header. The format of the header is always the same and you only need to change the relevant information for every plugin:

```php
<?php
/*
Plugin Name: WP Digg This
Version: 0.1
Description: Automatically adds Digg This button to your posts.
Author: Vladimir Prelovac
Author URI: http://www.prelovac.com/vladimir
Plugin URI: http://www.prelovac.com/vladimir/wordpress-plugins/
wp-digg-this
*/
?>
```

3. Now add the code to check the WordPress version:

```php
/* Version check */
global $wp_version;

$exit_msg='WP Digg This requires WordPress 2.5 or newer.
<a href="http://codex.wordpress.org/Upgrading_WordPress">Please
update!</a>';
```

```
if (version_compare($wp_version,"2.5","<"))
{
    exit ($exit_msg);
}
?>
```

4. Upload your plugin file to the `wp-content/plugins` folder on your server using your FTP client.

5. Go to your WordPress **Plugins** admin panel. You should now see your plugin listed among other plugins:

Plugin Management

Plugins extend and expand the functionality of WordPress. Once a plugin is installed, you may a

Plugin	Version	Description
Akismet	2.1.4	Akismet checks your comments against the Akismet web service to see if they look like spam or not. You need a WordPress.com API key to use it. You can review the spam it catches under "Comments." To show off your Akismet stats just put <?php akismet_counter(); ?> in your template. See also: WP Stats plugin. *By Matt Mullenweg.*
Hello Dolly	1.5	This is not just a plugin, it symbolizes the hope and enthusiasm of an entire generation summed up in two words sung most famously by Louis Armstrong: Hello, Dolly. When activated you will randomly see a lyric from Hello, Dolly in the upper right of your admin screen on every page. *By Matt Mullenweg.*
WP Digg This	0.1	Automatically adds Digg This button to your posts. *By Vladimir Prelovac.*

6. This means we have just completed the necessary steps to display our plugin in WordPress. Our plugin can be even activated now—although it does not do anything useful (yet).

What just happened?

We created a working plugin template by using a plugin information header and the version check code. The plugin header allows the plugin to be identified and displayed properly in the plugins admin panel. The version check code will warn users of our plugin who have older WordPress versions to upgrade their WordPress installation and prevent compatibility problems.

The plugin information header

To identify the plugin to WordPress, we need to include a plugin information header with each plugin.

The header is written as a PHP comment and contains several fields with important information.

This code alone is enough for the plugin to be registered, displayed in the admin panel and readied for activation.

If your future plugin has more than one PHP file, the plugin information should be placed only in your main file, the one which will include() or require() the other plugin PHP files.

Checking WordPress versions

To ensure that our plugin is not activated on incompatible WordPress versions, we will perform a simple WordPress version check at the very beginning of our code.

WordPress provides the global variable $wp_version that provides the current WordPress version in standard format. We can then use PHP function version_compare() to compare this and our required version for the plugin, using the following code:

```
if (version_compare($wp_version,"2.6","<"))
{
    // do something if WordPress version is lower then 2.6
}
```

If we want to stop the execution of the plugin upon activation, we can use the exit() function with the error message we want to show.

In our case, we want to show the required version information and display the link to the WordPress upgrade site.

```
$exit_msg='WP Digg This requires WordPress 2.6 or newer. <a
href="http://codex.wordpress.org/Upgrading_WordPress">Please
update!</a>';
```

```
if (version_compare($wp_version,"2.6","<"))
{
    exit ($exit_msg);
}
```

While being simple, this piece of code is also very effective. With the constant development of WordPress, and newer versions evolving relatively often, you can use version checking to prevent potential incompatibility problems.

The version number of your current WordPress installation can be found in the footer text of the admin menu. To begin with, you can use that version in your plugin version check (for example 2.6).

Later, when you learn about WordPress versions and their differences, you'll be able to lower the version requirement to the minimal your plugin will be compatible with. This will allow your plugin to be used on more blogs, as not all blogs always use the latest version of WordPress.

Checking the plugin

You can go ahead and activate the plugin. The plugin will be activated but will do nothing at this moment.

Time for Action – Testing the version check

Let's just make sure that the version check works, by requiring a fictional version of WordPress that does not exist yet:

1. Deactivate the plugin and change the version check code to a higher version. For example, replace 2.6 with 5.0.

   ```
   if (version_compare($wp_version,"5.0","<"))
   ```

2. Re-upload the plugin and try to activate it again. You will see a WordPress error and a message from the plugin:

What just happened?

The version check fails and the plugin exits with our predefined error message. The same thing will happen to a user trying to use your plugin with outdated WordPress installation, requiring them to update to a newer version.

Have a go Hero

We created a basic plugin that you can now customize.

- ◆ Change the plugin description to include HTML formatting (add **bold** or links to the description).

- ◆ Test your plugin to see what happens if you have two plugins with the same name (upload a copy of the file under a different name).

Displaying a Digg button

Now it's time to expand our plugin with concrete functionality and add a **Digg** link to every post on our blog.

In order to create a link we will need to extract post's permalink URL, title, and description. Luckily, WordPress provides us with a variety of ways to do this.

Time for Action – Implement a Digg link

Let's create a function to display a **Digg submit** link using information from the post.

Then we will implement this function into our theme, to show the link just after the post content.

1. Add a function to our plugin to display a **Digg** link:

```
/* Show a Digg This link */
function WPDiggThis_Link()
{
    global $post;
    // get the URL to the post
    $link=urlencode(get_permalink($post->ID));

    // get the post title
    $title=urlencode($post->post_title);
    // get first 350 characters of post and strip it off
    // HTML tags
```

```
$text=urlencode(substr(strip_tags($post->post_content),
                                            0, 350));
// create a Digg link and return it
return '<a href="http://digg.com/submit?url='.$link.'&amp;
    title='.$title.'&amp;bodytext='.$text.'">Digg This</a>';
}
```

2. Open your theme's `single.php` file and add a call to our function just below the line with `the_content()`. If you are not sure how to do this, see the forthcoming section on "Editing the theme files".

```
<?php if (function_exists(WPDiggThis_Link)) echo WPDiggThis_
                                            Link(); ?>
```

3. With the default WordPress theme, this change will look something like this (you can also refer to the following image):

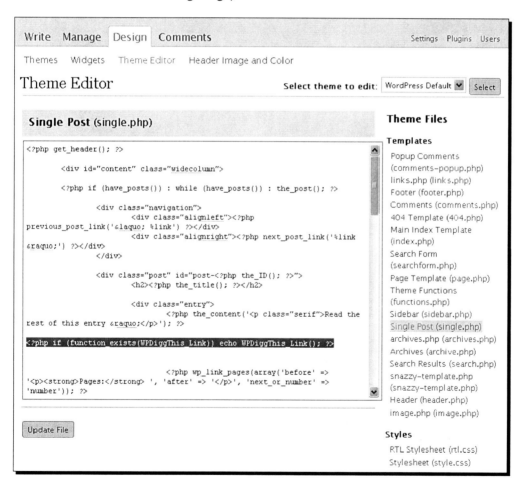

4. After you save the theme file, your blog posts will now automatically have the **Digg This** link shown after the content:

New WordPress plugin WP Digg This

The cool new WordPress plugin allows the user to easily add the Digg This functionality to their blog.

This post is used to test the functionality of the plugin.

Digg This

5. Clicking the link will take the user directly to the Digg site, with all the required information already filled in:

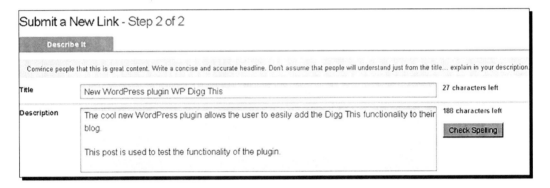

Well done! You have created your first working WordPress plugin!

What just happened?

When WordPress loads a post, the `single.php` template file from the currently active WordPress theme is ran. We added a line to this file that calls our plugin function `WPDiggThis_Link()` just after the content of the post is displayed:

```php
<?php the_content('<p class="serif">Read the rest of this entry &raquo;</p>'); ?>

<?php if (function_exists(WPDiggThis_Link)) echo WPDiggThis_Link(); ?>
```

We use `function_exists()` to check our function because it exists only if our plugin is installed and activated. PHP will generate an error if we try to run a nonexistent function. But if we deactivate the plugin later, we don't want to cause errors with our theme. So, we make sure that the function exists before we attempt to run it.

Assuming that the plugin is present and activated, the WPDiggThis_Link() function from our plugin is ran. The first part of the following function gets information about our post and assigns it to variables:

```
/* Show a Digg This link */
function WPDiggThis_Link()
{
    global $post;

    // get the URL to the post
    $link=urlencode(get_permalink($post->ID));

    // get the post title
    $title=urlencode($post->post_title);

    // get first 350 characters of post and strip it off HTML tags
    $text=urlencode(substr(strip_tags($post->post_content),
                                          0, 350));
```

We use the urlencode() PHP function for all the parameters that we will pass to the final link. This will ensure that all the values are formatted properly.

The second part uses this information to construct a **Digg submit** link:

```
    // create a Digg link and return it
    return '<a href="http://digg.com/submit?url='.$link.'&amp;
       title='.$amp;title.'&bodytext='.$text.'">Digg This</a>';

}
```

It returns this HTML text so that it gets added to the WordPress output at the point where the function is called – just after the post is displayed. Therefore, the link appears right after each post—which is convenient for the user who has just finished reading the post.

Using the Digg API

Usually, when using the functionalities of third-party sites, as we are doing in our example with Digg, we would search for the API documentation first. Almost all the major sites have extensive documentation available to help developers use their services in an effective way.

Digg is no exception, and if you search the Internet for the **digg button api** you will find a page at http://digg.com/tools/integrate that will have all the details we need in order to implement our Digg functionality.

Digg allows us to use several different ways of using their service.

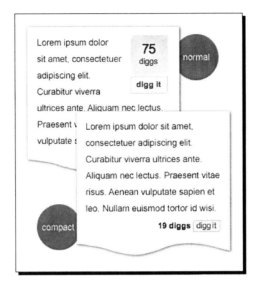

For the start, we will display just a Digg link. Later, we will expand it and also display a normal button.

Here is what the Digg documentation says about formatting a submit link.

Submit URL:

```
http://digg.com/submit?url=example.com&title=TITLE&bodytext=DESCRIPTI
ON&media=MEDIA&topic=TOPIC
```

Submit URL Details:

♦ **url**=example.com

Maximum length is 255 characters

Story URL should be unique and devoid of session or user-specific data

Please URL-encode all strings as appropriate. For example:

```
http%3A%2F%2Fyourwebsite%2Fyourstoryurl%2Fstorypagedetails.html
```

♦ **title**=TITLE

Maximum length is 75 characters

Please also URL-encode the story title

♦ **bodytext**=DESCRIPTION

Maximum length is 350 characters

Please also URL-encode the body text

Using this information, we are able to create a valid link for the Digg service from the information available in our post.

Acquiring post information

WordPress provides a number of ways to get information about the current post.

One of them involves using the global variable `$post`, which stores all the relevant information for the current post. We have used it in our example to extract the post title and content, but it can also be used to get other information such as post category, status and so on.

WordPress also offers an array of functions we could have used to access post information such as `get_the_title()` and `get_the_content()`.

The main difference between using these functions and accessing post data directly using `$post` variable is in the end information we get. The `$post` variable contains raw information about the post, just as the user wrote it. The functions mentioned above take the same raw information as a starting point, but could have the final output modified by external factors such as other active plugins.

 You can browse through the `wp-includes/post-template.php` file of your WordPress installation to get a better understanding of the differences between using the `$post` variable and the WordPress provided functions.

Post permalink URL

In order to obtain post URL we used the `get_permalink()` WordPress function. This function accepts the post ID as a parameter, and as a result, returns post's actual URL on the blog. It will always return a valid URL to your post no matter what permalink structure your blog is using.

Editing the theme files

In our example, we had to edit our theme in order to place the Digg link under the post content. WordPress allows for easy theme editing through the built-in **Theme Editor** panel.

After selecting the theme you want to edit, you will be presented with a number of options. Every theme consists of various PHP template files, each covering different blog functionalities.

Here is a reference table detailing the most commonly used template files.

File	Page	Description
`index.php`	Main index file	This is the main theme file; it is used to render any page as a replacement if the 'specialised' file listed below is missing
`home.php`	Home page	Used to display the contents of the home page of the blog, which usually includes a list of recent posts.
`single.php`	Single post	Called when you click on a single post to display post comments; usually includes comments template at the end.
`page.php`	Page Template	Same as single post, but is used for displaying pages
`archive.php`	Archives	Displays blog archives, such as earlier posts, posts by month or categories.
`comments.php`	Comments	Template responsible for showing user comments and the comment area for new comments
`header.php`	Header	Outputs the header for every page, usually containing information such as title and navigation, and includes theme style sheets and so on
`footer.php`	Footer	The footer of every page, usually containing copyright information and useful links
`search.php`	Search results	This template is used to show search results for your blog; It is usually similar to archive.php but also includes information about the searched-for phrase
`sidebar.php`	Sidebar	Shows the blog sidebar; if the theme supports widgets, it will also include widget support functions
`404.php`	404 file not found page	Default page for showing missing (404) pages on your blog

Always be careful when editing the theme files as any kind of mistake in your syntax can cause an error in displaying the page. It is therefore good practice to first backup theme files, so you can safely revert to them afterwards.

Quick reference

$post: A global WordPress variable containing information about the currently processed post.

get_permalink($post_id): Returns the full URL to the post given by its ID (for example $post->ID).

function_exists($function): Helps the PHP function to check if the given function exists. It is useful in themes when we want to include our function.

urlencode($string): Helps the PHP function to properly format the parameters to be used in a URL query.

Have a go Hero

Our plugin already has useful functionality. Try to customize it by:

- Calling our Digg link function from different places in the theme template, for example, before the content or after the tags are displayed (look for the_tags() line in the template).

- Adding the function to other theme templates such as the main index file and archive pages to display the Digg links on the home page and blog archives as well.

- Using the get_the_title() and get_the_content() functions to obtain post title and content instead of using the $post variable.

WordPress plugin hooks

Our plugin now works fine, but there is a problem. In order to use it, we also have to edit the theme. This can be a real pain for all sorts of reasons:

- If you want to change to a different theme, the plugin will stop working until you edit the new theme.

- If you want to distribute your plugin to other people, they can't just install it and activate it; they have to change their theme files too.

- If you change the function name, you need to alter the theme files again

We need some way to make the plugin work on its own, without the users having to change their themes or anything else.

Hooks come to the rescue, making it possible to display our **Digg This** button in our posts—without ever modifying our theme.

Time for Action – Use a filter hook

We will use the `the_content` filter hook to automatically add our **Digg This** link to the end of the post content. This will avoid the need for the users to edit their theme files if they want to use our plugin.

1. Create a function that we will use to hook to the content filter:

```
// create a Digg link and return it
return '<a href="http://digg.com/submit?url='.$link.'&amp;
  title='.$title.'&amp;bodytext='.$text.'">Digg This</a>';
}


/* Add Digg link to the end of the post */
function WPDiggThis_ContentFilter($content)
{
    return $content.WPDiggThis_Link();
}
```

2. Use the post content hook to automatically call our new function:

```
add_filter('the_content', 'WPDiggThis_ContentFilter');
```

3. Remove the references to our function from the theme template as we no longer need them. Leaving them would have the effect of showing the link twice.

The end result is now the same, but we now control the appearance of the link directly from our plugin.

What just happened?

When we activate our plugin now, WordPress comes across and runs this line:

```
add_filter('the_content', 'WPDiggThis_ContentFilter');
```

This tells WordPress that every time it's going to display the content of a post or page, it should run it through our `WPDiggThis_ContentFilter()` function. We don't need to modify the theme file anymore – WordPress will make sure that the function runs at the required time.

When we load a post now, WordPress will automatically call our function:

```
/* Add Digg link to the end of the post */
function WPDiggThis_ContentFilter($content)
{
    return $content.WPDiggThis_Link();
}
```

This function receives the post's content as a parameter, and returns the **filtered** content. In this case, our Digg link gets automatically appended to the end of the content.

WordPress hooks

WordPress provides a powerful mechanism for plugin functions to be called at the exact time when we need them. This functionality is accomplished by using the so called **hooks**.

Every time you call a page from your browser, the WordPress engine goes through every possible function it needs to render the requested page. Somewhere along the way, you can "hook" up your function and use it to affect the end result.

You do this by simply registering your function with a specified hook, allowing it to be called by WordPress at the right moment.

There are two types of WordPress hooks:

- **Action hooks**: These are triggered by WordPress events, for example, when someone creates a post or writes a comment.
- **Filter hooks**: These are used to modify WordPress content on the fly, like title or content of the post as it is being served to the user.

Filter hooks

We learned that filter hooks (also referred to as simply 'filters') are functions that process WordPress content, whether it is about to be saved in the database or displayed in the user's browser. WordPress expects these functions to modify the content they get and return it.

In our case, we used `the_content` filter hook to modify the post content by appending a Digg link to it. We could also have placed the Digg link at the beginning of the post, or broken up the post and put it in the middle.

To set up a filter, we need to use the `add_filter` function:

```
add_filter ( 'filter_hook', 'filter_function_name' , [priority],
[accepted_args] );
```

- `filter_hook`: One of the filter hooks provided by WordPress.
- `filter_function_name`: A function used to process the content provided by the filter_hook.
- `priority`: An optional parameter, which specifies the execution order of functions. The default value is 10 if several functions apply to the same filter hook, functions with a lower priority number execute first, while the functions with the same priority will execute in the order in which they were added to the filter.

◆ `accepted_args`: An optional parameter, which specifies how many arguments your function can accept. The default value is 1. The `accepted_args` parameter is used for hooks that pass more than one argument.

Here is an example list of filter hooks, which will help you to get a better understanding of what you can achieve using them.

Filter	Description
`the_content`	Applied to the post content retrieved from the database prior to printing on the screen
`the_content_rss`	Applied to the post content prior to including in an RSS feed
`the_title`	Applied to the post title retrieved from the database prior to printing on the screen
`wp_title`	Applied to the blog page title before sending to the browser in the `wp_title` function
`comment_text`	Applied to the comment text before display on the screen by the `comment_text` function and in the admin menus
`get_categories`	Applied to the category list generated by the `get_categories` function
`the_permalink`	Applied to the permalink URL for a post prior to printing by the `the_permalink` function
`autosave_interval`	Applied to the interval for auto-saving posts
`theme_root_uri`	Applied to the theme root directory URI returned by the `get_theme_root_uri` function

Filter hooks can be removed using the `remove_filter()` function. It accepts the same arguments as `add_filter()`, and is useful if you want to replace some of the existing WordPress filters with your functions.

If you want to take a closer look at the default WordPress filters, you can find them in the `wp-includes\default-filters.php` file of your WordPress installation.

 It is important to remember that the filter function always receives some data and is responsible for returning the data, whether it modifies the data or not. Only if you want to disregard this data completely, can you return an empty value.

Action hooks

We use action hooks when we need to include specific functionalities every time a WordPress event triggers, for example when the user publishes a post or changes the theme.

WordPress does not ask for any information back from the action function, it simply notifies it that a certain event has happened, and that a function should respond to it in a desired way.

Action hooks are used in a way similar to the filter hooks. The syntax for setting up an action hooks is:

```
add_action ( 'action_hook', 'action_function_name', [priority],
[accepted_args] );
```

◆ `action_hook`: The name of the hook provided by WordPress.

◆ `action_function_name`: The name of the function you want to use to handle the event.

◆ `priority`: An optional parameter, which specifies the execution order of functions. The default value is 10. If several functions apply to the same filter hook, then functions with lower priority numbers will execute first, while the functions with the same priority will execute in the order in which they were added.

◆ `accepted_args`: It is optional and specifies how many arguments your function can accept. The default value is 1 and is used for hooks that pass more than one argument.

The following table presents example action hooks provided by WordPress.

Action	Description
`create_category`	Runs when a new category is created
`publish_post`	Runs when a post is published, or if it is edited and its status is `published`
`wp_blacklist_check`	Runs to check whether a comment should be blacklisted
`switch_theme`	Runs when the blog's theme is changed
`activate_ (plugin_file_name)`	Runs when the plugin is first activated
`admin_head`	Runs in the HTML `<head>` section of the admin panel
`wp_head`	Runs when the template calls the `wp_head` function. This hook is generally placed near the top of a page template between `<head>` and `</head>`
`init`	Runs after WordPress has finished loading but before any headers are sent; it is useful for intercepting `$_GET` or `$_POST` triggers
`user_register`	Runs when a user's profile is first created

Just as with filters, you can use the `remove_action()` function to remove currently registered actions.

Practical filters and actions examples

Since understanding the power of filters and actions is very important for conquering WordPress plugin development, we will now examine a few more simple examples of their usage.

Upper case titles

The hook function can be any registered function. In this case, we will pass the title of the post to `strtoupper` making all titles appear in upper case.

```
add_filter('the_title', strtoupper);
```

Mailing list

Actions provide a very powerful mechanism for automating tasks. Here is how to send a notification to a mailing list whenever there is an update on your blog.

```
function mailing_list($post_ID)
{
    $list = 'john@somesite.com,becky@somesite.com';
    mail($list, 'My Blog Update',
        'My blog has just been updated: '.get_settings('home'));
}
// Send notification with every new post and comment
add_action('publish_post', 'mailing_list');
add_action('comment_post', 'mailing_list');
```

Changing core WordPress functionality

Sometimes you may not be satisfied with the default WordPress functionalities. You may be tempted to modify the WordPress source code, but you should never do that. One of the main reason is that when you upgrade to a new version of WordPress the upgrade process could overwrite your changes.

Instead, try whenever possible to write a plugin and use actions and filters to change the desired functionality.

Let's say we want to change WordPress post excerpt handling. WordPress uses the `wp_trim_excerpt()` function with the `get_the_excerpt` filter responsible for processing the post excerpt. No problem, let's replace it with our own function, using the WordPress function as a starting point.

```
/* Create excerpt with 70 words and preserved HTML tags */
function my_wp_trim_excerpt($text)
{
    if ( '' == $text )
    {
        $text = get_the_content('');
        $text = apply_filters('the_content', $text);
        $text = str_replace(']]>', ']]&gt;', $text);
        $excerpt_length = 70;
        $words = explode(' ', $text, $excerpt_length + 1);
        if (count($words) > $excerpt_length)
        {
            array_pop($words);
            array_push($words, '[...]');
            $text = implode(' ', $words);
        }
    }
    return $text;
}
// remove WordPress default excerpt filter
remove_filter('get_the_excerpt', 'wp_trim_excerpt');
// Add our custom filter with low priority
add_filter('get_the_excerpt', my_wp_trim_excerpt, 20);
```

These were just a few practical examples. You can do almost anything that crosses your mind using action and filter hooks in WordPress.

Sometimes, you can achieve the same result by using either the action or the filter hook.

For example, if you want to change the text of the post you can use `publish_post` action hook to change the post as it is being saved to the database.

Alternatively, you can use `the_content` filter to change the text of the post as it is displayed in the browser window.

Although the result is the same, we accomplish the goal in different ways. In the first case, when using the action hook, the post itself will remain permanently changed, whereas using the filter hook will change the text every time it is displayed. You will want to use the functionality more suitable for your needs.

Quick reference

```
add_filter ('filter_hook', 'filter_function_name',
[priority], [accepted_args]):
```
This is used to hook our function to the given filter

```
add_action ('action_hook', 'action_function_name',
[priority], [accepted_args]):
```
This is used to hook our function to the given action

`remove_filter()` and `remove_action()`: This is used to remove already assigned filters and actions

`the_content` : This is a popular filter for the post content. (do not confuse with `the_content()` function, which is a template tag to display the content of a post in the theme)

WordPress Filter Reference: `http://codex.wordpress.org/Plugin_API/Filter_Reference`

WordPress Action Reference: `http://codex.wordpress.org/Plugin_API/Action_Reference`

Have a go Hero

Our filter function now controls the behaviour of a Digg link. Try these exercises:

- Place a Digg link before the post content by prepending the output of our function to the content

- Add the current date to your page title in the browser window by using the `wp_title` filter and the `date()` PHP function

- Capitalize the first letter of the users' comments in case they forgot to do so. Use the `comment_text` filter and the `ucfirst()` PHP function

Adding a Digg button using JavaScript code

Our Digg link works fine for submitting the content, but isn't very pretty, and does not show the number of Diggs we received. That is why we need to use a standard **Digg** button.

This is accomplished by using a simple piece of JavaScript code provided by Digg, and passing it the necessary information.

Time for Action – Implement a Digg button

Let us implement a **Digg** button, using information from the Digg API. We will use the newly created button on single posts, and keep the simple **Digg** link for all the other pages.

1. Create a new function for displaying a nice **Digg** button using JavaScript code.

```
/* Return a Digg button */
function WPDiggThis_Button()
{
    global $post;

    // get the URL to the post
    $link=js_escape(get_permalink($post->ID));

    // get the post title
    $title=js_escape($post->post_title);

    // get the content
    $text=js_escape(substr(strip_tags($post->post_content),
                                             0, 350));

    // create a Digg button and return it
        $button="
        <script type='text/javascript'>
        digg_url = '$link';
        digg_title = '$title';
        digg_bodytext = '$text';
        </script>
    <script src='http://digg.com/tools/diggthis.js'
            type='text/javascript'></script>"
 return ($button);
}
```

2. Modify our filter function to include the **Digg** button for single posts and pages, and a Digg link for all the other pages:

```
/* Add Digg This to the post */
function WPDiggThis_ContentFilter($content)
{
// if on single post or page display the button
if (is_single() || is_page())
        return WPDiggThis_Button().$content;
    else
        return $content.WPDiggThis_Link();
}
```

3. **Digg** button now shows at the beginning of the single post page.

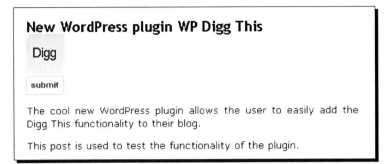

What just happened?

WordPress will parse our content filter function according to the conditional statement we have added:

```
function WPDiggThis_ContentFilter($content)
{
    // if on single post or page display the button
    if (is_single() || is_page())
     return WPDiggThis_Button().$content;
```

This means that if the current viewed page is a single post or page, we will append our **Digg** button at the beginning of that post.

If we are viewing all the other pages on the blog (like for example the home page or archives) we will show the **Digg This** link instead.

```
    if (is_single() || is_page())
        return WPDiggThis_Button().$content;
    else
        return $content.WPDiggThis_Link();
}
```

The reason for doing so is that we do not want to clutter the home page of the blog with a lot of big yellow Digg buttons. So we just place a subtle link below the post instead. On single pages, we show the normal button using our new `WPDiggThis_Button()` function.

The first part is similar to our previous `WPDiggThis_Link()` function, and it acquires the necessary post information.

```
/* Return a Digg button */
function WPDiggThis_Button()
{
    global $post;
    // get the URL to the post
    $link=js_escape(get_permalink($post->ID));
    // get the post title
    $title=js_escape($post->post_title);
    // get the content
    $text=js_escape(substr(strip_tags($post->post_content), 0, 350));
```

However in this case, we are treating all the information through the `js_escape()` WordPress function, which handles formatting of content for usage in JavaScript code. This includes handling of quotes, double quotes and line endings, and is necessary to make sure that our JavaScript code will work properly.

We then create a code using Digg API documentation for a JavaScript button:

```
// create a Digg button and return it
    $button="
    <script type='text/javascript'>
    digg_url = '$link';
    digg_title = '$title';
    digg_bodytext = '$text';
    </script>
    <script src='http://digg.com/tools/diggthis.js'
                type='text/javascript'></script>";
```

Conditional Tags

We have used two functions in our example, `is_single()` and `is_page()`. These are WordPress conditional tags and are useful for determining the currently viewed page on the blog. We used them to determine if we want to display a button or just a link.

WordPress provides a number of conditional tags that can be used to control execution of your code depending on what the user is currently viewing.

Here is the reference table for some of the most popular conditional tags.

Tag	Returns True If User is Viewing
is_home	Blog home page
is_admin	Administration interface
is_single	Single post page
is_page	Blog page
is_category	Archives by category
is_tag	Archives by tag
is_date	Archives by date
is_search	Search results

Conditional tags are used in a variety of ways. For example, is_single('15') checks whether the current page is a single post with ID 15. You can also check by title. is_page('About') checks if we are on the page with the title 'About'.

Quick reference

is_single(), is_page(): These are conditional tags to determine the nature of the currently viewed content

js_escape(): A WordPress function to properly escape the strings to be used in JavaScript code

WordPress Conditional Tags: http://codex.wordpress.org/Conditional_Tags

Styling the output

Our **Digg** button looks like it could use a better positioning, as the default one spoils the look of the theme. So, we will use CSS to reposition the button.

Cascading Style Sheets or CSS for short (http://www.w3.org/Style/CSS/) are a simple but powerful tool that allows web developers to add different styles to web presentations. They allow full control over the layout, size and colour of elements on a given page.

Time for Action – Use CSS to position the button

Using CSS styles, we will move the button to the right of the post.

1. We will accomplish this by first encapsulating the button in a <div> element. Then we will add a CSS style to this element stating that the button should appear on the right, with a left margin towards the text of 10 pixels.

```
// create a Digg button and return it
$button="
<script type='text/javascript'>
digg_url = '$link';
digg_title = '$title';
digg_bodytext = '$text';
</script>
<script src='http://digg.com/tools/diggthis.js' type='text/
                                    javascript'></script>";

// encapsulate the button in a div
$button='
    <div style="float: right; margin-left:
              10px; margin-bottom: 4px;">
'.$button.'
</div>';
```

```
    return $button;
```

2. The result of applying this simple CSS code is that **Digg** Button now shows to the right of the post.

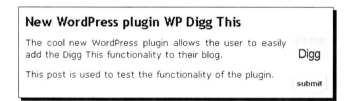

What just happened?

We used CSS to move the button to a desired position. CSS is extremely useful for these kinds of tasks and is commonly used in WordPress development to enhance the user experience.

```
// encapsulate the button in a div
$button='
    <div style="float: right; margin-left: 10px; margin-bottom:
4px;">
'.$button.'
</div>';
```

We have basically encapsulated our button in a `<div>` element and forced it to the right edge by using `float: right` CSS command inside a `style` tag.

We could further experiment with the placement of the button until we find the most satisfying solution.

For example, if we hook to `the_title` filter instead of `the_content`, and moved the button to the left, we would get the following result:

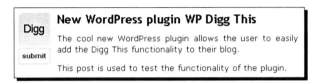

Certainly, having good CSS skills is a very valuable asset in WordPress plugin development.

Have a go Hero

Now that our button is finished, there are a lot of possible customizations you can make to the look or position of your button, using both built-in Digg options and CSS.

◆ You can use the `digg_bgcolor`, `digg_skin`, `digg_window` parameters of Digg JavaScript to control the appearance of the button (refer to `http://digg.com/tools/integrate`)

◆ Use CSS to play with the layout of the button

◆ Create similar plugins that will allow the user to submit content to sites such as Stumble Upon or Reddit

Summary

In this chapter, we created a working, useful, and attractive WordPress plugin from scratch. Our plugin now displays a fully functional **Digg** button.

We learned how to extract information using WordPress API and how to use CSS to improve the appearance of our plugin. We also investigated some more advanced WordPress functionalities such as hooks.

Specifically, we covered:

◆ **Creating a plugin**: How to fill in the information header and create a simple plugin template

◆ **Checking WordPress version**: How to check that our plugin is compatible with the user's version of WordPress

◆ **Modifying theme files**: How to safely add functions to the theme files when we need to

- **Accessing post information**: Different ways of obtaining data from the post such as title, permalink and content

- **Using WordPress hooks**: How to use actions and filters to get things done from within our plugin (and not modifying the theme for instance)

Now that we've learned about WordPress hooks, we are ready to expand our knowledge and learn about **Widgets**. In the next chapter we will create a cool Wall widget for users to write comments directly on our blog sidebar.

3
Live Blogroll

We learned how to set up a fully functional WordPress plugin, and use WordPress hooks to insert our code exactly when we want it.

In this chapter, we will move on and explore more cool things we can do with WordPress by livening up the default WordPress Blogroll.

The purpose of the plugin will be to display the most recent posts from the sites listed in the blogroll using a nice pop-up window. We also want to do that dynamically, using Ajax and jQuery technologies.

Do not worry if you know little about them right now. They integrate naturally with WordPress, and soon you'll consider them as being part of WordPress!

In this chapter, you will:

- Use more hooks, more **API** features
- Deal with **RSS,** an important aspect of blogging
- Get familiar with **jQuery** and **Ajax,** and load the 'recent posts' dynamically
- Learn how to make the plugin secure by using nonces

You will learn this by:

- Creating a live **Blogroll** plugin that adds a 'recent posts' pop up for each blog in your blogroll

The integrated WordPress Blogroll is very rudimentary one; it just displays a list of links that stay exactly the same over time. Here is what it normally looks like:

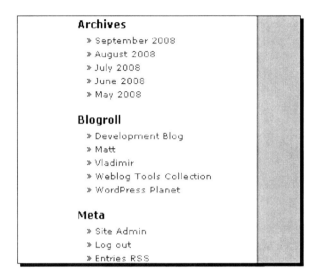

What if it could give us an insight into what is happening on the site by showing the most recent posts?

Our plugin makes this functionality possible, is attractive to use, and will not slow down the loading time of the main page. We will call the plugin 'Live Blogroll' as this is what it will actually do—breathe life into our blogroll!

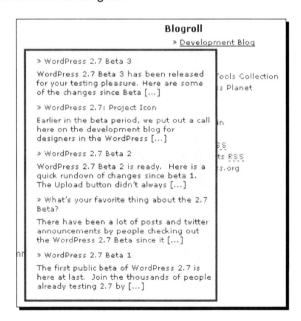

Starting up with the blogroll

The WordPress Blogroll is a collection of links to other sites. You can manage these links in the WordPress administration menu where you can add, modify, and delete them. The changes are represented instantaneously on your **Blogroll** and are visible to the visitors of your site.

WordPress allow us to hook up into the process of preparing the blogroll links just before they are displayed on the site. We will use this as a first step in our plugin, to demonstrate how to fetch the RSS feed from the link and display the title of the first post as a link.

This will make the blogroll look livelier as it will constantly change with the posting of new articles on those sites.

Archives
» September 2008
» August 2008
» July 2008
» June 2008
» May 2008

Blogroll
» WordPress 2.7 Beta 3
» NYTimes Sleep
» Official Google Search Engine Optimization Guide
» WordPress Plugin Releases for 11/16
» Weblog Tools Collection: WordPress Plugin Releases for 11/16

Meta
» Site Admin
» Log out
» Entries RSS

Time for action – Roll into the blogroll

We want to hook up into the blogroll filter and modify the links on the fly, fetching the latest post from the RSS feed and replacing it into the blogroll.

1. Create a new folder for the plugin, called `live-blogroll`. We will have more than one file in our final plugin, so that we can keep everything neatly in one folder.

2. Create a new file called `wp-live-blogroll.php`. This will be our main file and should contain the plugin information. We can also re-use our version check code:

```php
<?php
/*
Plugin Name: Live Blogroll
Version: 0.1
Description: Shows a number of 'recent posts' for each link in
your Blogroll using Ajax.
Author: Vladimir Prelovac
Author URI: http://www.prelovac.com/vladimir
Plugin URI: http://www.prelovac.com/vladimir/wordpress-plugins/
live-blogroll
*/

/* Version check */
global $wp_version;

$exit_msg='Live BlogRoll requires WordPress 2.3 or newer.
<a href="http://codex.wordpress.org/Upgrading_WordPress">Please
update!</a>';
if (version_compare($wp_version,"2.3","<"))
{
    exit ($exit_msg);
}

?>
```

3. We will also define a plugin path that we will use later:

```php
$wp_live_blogroll_plugin_url = trailingslashit
WP_PLUGIN_DIR.'/'. dirname
( plugin_basename(__FILE__) );
```

4. Include the `rss.php` file, which contains functions, which are needed for parsing RSS feeds:

```php
require_once(ABSPATH . WPINC . '/rss.php');
```

5. Next, we want to hook to `get_bookmarks` in order to change the blogroll display:

```php
add_filter('get_bookmarks', WPLiveRoll_GetBookmarksFilter);
```

6. Now, let's add the filter function:

```
function WPLiveRoll_GetBookmarksFilter($items)
{
    // do nothing if in the admin menu
  if (is_admin())
  {
    return $items;
  }

  // parse all blogroll items
  foreach($items as $item)
  {
    // check if the link is public
    if ($item->link_visible=='Y')
    {
      $link_url=trailingslashit($item->link_url);

      // simple feed guessing
      if (strstr($link_url,"blogspot"))
      {
        // blogspot blog
        $feed_url=$link_url."feeds/posts/default/";
      }
      else if (strstr($link_url,"typepad"))
      {
        // typepad blog
        $feed_url=$link_url."atom.xml";
      }
      else
      {
        // own domain or wordpress blog
        $feed_url=$link_url."feed/";
      }

      // use WordPress to fetch the RSS feed
      $feedfile = fetch_rss($feed_url);

      // check if we got valid response
      if (is_array($feedfile->items )
      && !empty($feedfile->items ) )
      {
        // this is the last post
        $feeditem=$feedfile->items[0];
        // replace name and url with post link and title
        $item->link_url=$feeditem['link'];
        $item->link_name=$feeditem['title'];
      }
```

```
        }
    }
    // return the items back
    return $items;
}
```

7. Upload your whole plugin folder `live-blogroll` to the `wp-content/plugins` folder on your server.

8. Activate the plugin and check your blogroll. The new blogroll is shown with a fresh new look which displays all the latest posts.

What just happened?

When the page is loaded, the `get_bookmarks` filter is executed:

```
add_filter('get_bookmarks', WPLiveRoll_GetBookmarksFilter);
```

At this point, our filter function `WPLiveRoll_GetBookmarksFilter()` takes care of the blogroll processing:

```
function WPLiveRoll_GetBookmarksFilter($items)
{
    // do nothing if in the admin menu
    if (is_admin())
    {
        return $items;
    }
```

Since the `get_bookmarks` filter is activated on the administration pages (where we do not want to do anything), we are making a check by using the conditional tag `is_admin`. It will return true if the user is currently viewing the admin panel pages, in which case, we simply return the unprocessed items.

Next, we loop through all the links in the blogroll, and check to see if they are enabled:

```
        // parse all blogroll items
        foreach($items as $item)
        {
            // check if the link is public
            if ($item->link_visible=='Y')
            {
```

Now, when we have a published link we need to find the RSS feed from the site.

A detailed approach would involve loading the content of the page and processing it for the `<link>` tags and searching for one of the possible RSS formats.

For the purpose of this example, we will keep it simple by guessing the feed based on the site name, which will work for most blogs (you can develop a more comprehensive RSS discovery function as an exercise):

```
$link_url=trailingslashit($item->link_url);

// simple feed guessing
if (strstr($link_url,"blogspot.com"))
{
  // blogspot blog
  $feed_url=$link_url."feeds/posts/default/";
}
else
if (strstr($link_url,"typepad.com"))
{
  // typepad blog
  $feed_url=$link_url."atom.xml";
}
else
{
  // own domain or wordpress blog
  $feed_url=$link_url."feed/";
}
```

Now that we have the feed URL, we can fetch the contents of the feed using the WordPress function `fetch_rss()`:

```
// use WordPress to fetch the RSS feed
$feedfile = fetch_rss($feed_url);
```

The result should be an array of objects; each one representing information about a single post sorted by date.

First, we check to see if we get a valid response,

```
// check if we got valid response
if (is_array($feedfile->items )
&& !empty($feedfile->items ) )
{
```

And then replace the blogroll URL and name with latest post's URL and title:

```
// this is the last post
$feeditem=$feedfile->items[0];
// replace name and url with post link
  and title
  $item->link_url=$feeditem['link'];
```

```
            $item->link_name=$feeditem['title'];
        }
      }
    }
    // return the items back
    return $items;
}
```

In the end we return the items. Note that if we do not get a valid response, the original link will stay intact. It is a very simple automatic fallback in case we cannot parse the feed for some reason.

Our code needs RSS functionality, which comes through the `rss.php` file of the WordPress installation:

```
require_once(ABSPATH . WPINC . '/rss.php');
```

We included it using two WordPress defines, `ABSPATH` and `WPINC`, which contain the absolute path to the WordPress installation and the path to the WordPress includes folder.

Quick reference

`fetch_rss()`: Parses RSS feed, and requires rss.php file to be included.

`is_admin()`: Checks to see if the current page is an administration page.

`ABSPATH`: A variable which contains the absolute path to WordPress installation.

`WPINC`: A variable which contains the name of the includes folder.

`get_bookmarks`: A filter used to parse blogroll items.

`WP_PLUGIN_URL`: Contains the URL to the WordPress plugin folder

RSS Feed Processing

WordPress provides a very easy to use function, `fetch_rss()`, to process the RSS feeds. The function relies internally on RSS feed library that comes included with WordPress, and takes care of the all the related work.

The function returns an array of feed items, which you can easily loop through to extract the information you need:

```
$feedfile = fetch_rss($feed_url);

foreach($feedfile->items as $item )
{
```

You may have noticed a pause when loading the blogroll for the first time. This is caused by the fetching of the feeds and is especially noticeable if you have many links in your blogroll.

This delay exists only for the first time when new feeds are parsed. The RSS library has a built-in mechanism for caching the feeds. That means that for the next request, the feed will be served from the local cache if it has not been updated in the meantime.

The method we use is simple and effective, but now we want more interactivity. We do not want any delay in loading; we want to show more recent posts, and show them in a pop-up window. In order to achieve all this, we need to use a language specifically written to handle events on a web page—JavaScript.

jQuery JavaScript library

There are a number of libraries available which simplify the usage of JavaScript by providing ready-made functions for the most common tasks. The most popular today are jQuery, Scriptaculous and MooTools. WordPress comes with the first two pre-installed, and we will be using jQuery for our plugins.

Implementing a mouse hover event in jQuery

Although our plugin is fine, we would like it to interact with the user and show them the information when they want it, and where they want it. Responding to the user hovering the mouse over the link on the blogroll sounds like a good place to start.

Let's create a jQuery JavaScript that will show additional information in the blogroll, using the hover event as a trigger.

Time for action – Creating a hover event with jQuery

We will create an external file to store our JavaScript and use it to display a message directly in the blogroll, when the user hovers the mouse over one of the links.

1. Create a new file called `wp-live-blogroll.js`.

2. Initialize jQuery when our page loads:

```
// setup everything when document is ready
jQuery(document).ready(function($)
{
```

3. Assign a hover event to our links.

```
// connect to hover event of <a> in .livelinks
$('.livelinks a').hover(function(e)
{
```

4. Insert a new element (`<div>`) on the mouse hover event. It will display a simple message for now (**Recent posts will be displayed here**) :

```
// set the text we want to display
this.tip="Recent posts from " + this.href + "
will be displayed here...";
// create a new div and display a tip inside
$(this).append('<div id="lb_popup">' + this.tip +
'</div>');
},
```

5. And remove it when the user moves the mouse:

```
// when the mouse hovers out
function()
{
    // remove it
    $(this).children().remove();
    });
});
```

6. Using jQuery we have just assigned hover event to class 'livelinks'.

That means that blogroll needs to be embedded within this class. Open up our plugin file `wp-live-blogroll.php` and add the following filter function to the end. It will embed our blogroll into the `livelinks` class.

```
add_filter('wp_list_bookmarks',
        WPLiveRoll_ListBookmarksFilter);

function WPLiveRoll_ListBookmarksFilter($content)
{
    return '<span class="livelinks">'.$content.'</span>';
}
```

7. Finally, we want to have WordPress load our script when the page loads.

We use the `wp_print_scripts` action to accomplish that and the `wp_enqueue_script` function to include our JavaScript:

```
add_action('wp_print_scripts', 'WPLiveRoll_ScriptsAction');
function WPLiveRoll_ScriptsAction()
{
  global $wp_live_blogroll_plugin_url;
  if (!is_admin())
  {
```

```
        wp_enqueue_script('jquery');
        wp_enqueue_script('wp_live_roll_script',
          $wp_live_blogroll_plugin_url.'/wp-live-blogroll.js',
          array('jquery'));
    }
  }
```

8. We do not want to use the get_bookmarks filter anymore. We will simply comment out the filter assignment:

```
add_filter('get_bookmarks', WPLiveRoll_GetBookmarksFilter);
```

9. Update the plugin on the server. Try to hover the mouse over one of the links and you should get our message.

Blogroll

» Development Blog
Recent posts from
http://wordpress.org
/development/ will be displayed
here...
» Matt
» Vladimir
» Weblog Tools Collection
» WordPress Planet

What just happened?

Our script is loaded in the <head> section of the page with the wp_print_scripts action, which is used to print out scripts our plugin will use.

```
add_action('wp_print_scripts', 'WPLiveRoll_ScriptsAction');
```

To actually add the scripts, we use the wp_enqueue_script() WordPress function, which will be covered in detail later. This function allows us to add preinstalled scripts like jQuery, or our custom scripts:

```
function WPLiveRoll_ScriptsAction()
{
  global $wp_live_blogroll_plugin_url;
  if (!is_admin())
  {
    wp_enqueue_script('jquery');
    wp_enqueue_script('wp_live_roll_script',
      $wp_live_blogroll_plugin_url.'/wp-live-blogroll.js',
      array('jquery'));
  }
}
```

Next, Blogroll is embedded in the `livelinks` class, so our jQuery code can properly assign the hover event. We used the `wp_list_bookmarks` hook, which executes just before the blogroll shows on the page.

```
add_filter('wp_list_bookmarks', WPLiveRoll_ListBookmarksFilter);
```

The filter function receives the full HTML code of the prepared blogroll, so we only need to embed its content into our `livelinks` class and return it:

```
function WPLiveRoll_ListBookmarksFilter($content)
{
    return '<span class="livelinks">'.$content.'</span>';
}
```

To work with jQuery when the page is ready, we need to initialize it at the beginning of the JavaScript code. jQuery provides the `ready` method which executes when the page is loaded (more accurately when the page code is loaded; the images may still be loading):

```
// set up everything when document is ready
jQuery(document).ready(function($)
{
```

Next, we set up a hover jQuery event for links inside the `livelinks` class using a jQuery selector (more on that later).

```
    // connect to hover event of <a> in .livelinks
    $('.livelinks a').hover(function(e)
    {
```

Now, we want to add a text and a `<div>` to display it in. We used the internal variable `this`, which represents the object that triggered the hover event (which will be one of the links in the Blogroll).

To store the temporary value of the text, we will create a new variable `tip` and use the URL of the link found in the link's `this.href` property:

```
        // set the text we want to display
        this.tip="Recent posts from " + this.href + "
        will be displayed here...";
```

We then dynamically append code to our link by using the jQuery `append()` method:

```
        // create a new div and display a tip inside
        $(this).append('<div id="lb_popup">' + this.tip +
            '</div>');
```

The hover event allows us to declare the function for handling the hover out event and we use it to remove the `<div>` when the user moves the mouse away from the link.

To do that, we can use the `children()` method, which references elements under our link, in this case, the appended div:

```
// when the mouse hovers out
function()
{
   // remove it
   $(this).children().remove();
}
});
```

JavaScript and WordPress

WordPress provides a way to add external scripts in an elegant way, by using the `wp_enqueue_script` function.

The `wp_enqueue_script` function is usually used in conjunction with the `wp_print_scripts` action and accepts up to four parameters: `handle`, `src`, `dependencies`, and `version`.

- ◆ `handle`: This is the name of the script, it should be a lowercase string.
- ◆ `src` (Optional): This is the path to the script from the root directory of WordPress, example: `/wp-includes/js/scriptaculous/scriptaculous.js`. This parameter is required only when WordPress does not already know about this script. It defaults to false.
- ◆ `dependencies` (Optional): This is an array of the handles of any scripts that this script depends on; which means, that the scripts that must be loaded before this script. Set it to false if there are no dependencies. This parameter is required only when WordPress does not already know about this script. It defaults to false.
- ◆ `version` (Optional): This is the string specifying a script version number, if it has one. It defaults to false. This parameter is used to ensure that the correct version is sent to the client regardless of caching, and should therefore be included if a version number is available and makes sense for the script.

In our example, we declared that we are using jQuery and then our own script by specifying the full path to it:

```
wp_enqueue_script('jquery');
wp_enqueue_script('wp_live_roll_script',
$wp_live_blogroll_plugin_url.'/wp-live-blogroll.js',
array('jquery'));
```

As mentioned before, WordPress comes preinstalled with a variety of scripts. To use them, you need to specify the handle to `wp_enqueue_script()`, as we did with jQuery. Some of the popular scripts included are **dbx** (**Docking Boxes**), colorpicker, `wp_tiny_mce` (**WordPress Tiny MCE**), autosave, scriptaculous, prototype, thickbox and others.

Quick reference

`wp_enqueue_script()`: This is used to queue an external script used by our plugin. Additional information is available at `http://codex.wordpress. org/Function_Reference/wp_enqueue_script`

`bloginfo()`: This is the function used to retrieve relevant blog information like the homepage URL and print it out. `get_bloginfo` also does the same thing; it only returns the information instead of printing it. More information is available at: `http://codex.wordpress.org/Template_Tags/ bloginfo`

`wp_print_scripts`: Filter which runs inside the `<head>` tag of the document, usually used to declare scripts

Initializing jQuery

We have initialized jQuery with this code:

```
// set up everything when document is ready
jQuery(document).ready(function($)
{
```

Notice the '`$`' parameter to the function? All jQuery variables and functions are constrained within the jQuery namespace. You can usually access them using `jQuery()` and also `$()`. The only problem is that sometimes other libraries also use `$` as their namespace reference, which leads to conflicts.

The most elegant way to avoid this is to declare the ready function as we did, which allows us to use the shorter `$` reference inside the `ready()` function while avoiding conflict with other libraries.

Expanding jQuery knowledge

One of the advantages of jQuery is the ability to access every single element in our document with ease. Let's try a few examples:

- `$("h1")`: gets all the `<h1>` tags
- `$("#sidebar")`: gets the element with `id="sidebar"`
- `$(".navigation")`: gets all the elements with `class="navigation"`

- ♦ $("div.post #image"): gets the element with id="image" nested in the <div class="post">
- ♦ $("#sidebar ul li"): gets all the <li> elements nested in all <ul>, under the element with id="sidebar"

More control is given with the commands such as first, last, contains, visible, for example:

- ♦ $("li:first"): selects the first instance
- ♦ $("li:contains(blog)"): selects all the elements in <li> that contain the text "blog"
- ♦ $("li:gt(n)"): selects all the elements in <li> with an index greater than (n)

Responding to user events is a breeze in jQuery. There are custom defined events that we can use such as: click, mouseover, hover, keydown, focus, and so on.

This code will add an alert pop-up whenever you click on any link on the page:

```
$(document).ready(function()
{
    $("a").click(function()
    {
        alert("Thanks for visiting!");
    });
});
```

jQuery allows us to modify the document by adding classes to the elements (addclass) or binding events to them easily.

```
$(document).ready(function()
{
    $('#button').bind('click', function(e)
    {
        alert('The mouse is now at ' + e.pageX + ', ' + e.pageY);
    });
});
```

jQuery also supports plugins, and there are literally hundreds of them which allows for almost any kind of effect or functionality that you may imagine.

 A good resource to start browsing for jQuery examples and documentation is the official web site at http://www.jquery.com and Learning jQuery web site at http://www.learningjquery.com.

Creating the pop-up with CSS

Let's move on with our plugin and create a pop-up window for our message. To do this, we will include CSS code and make a couple of changes to the plugin.

Time for action – Apply CSS to the popup

In this example, we are going to style our pop up using the CSS. The contents of the CSS will be located in the external file for easy editing. We will use another WordPress action to load this stylesheet from the `<head>` tag of the document.

1. Create a new file named `wp-live-blogroll.css`.

2. Add this code to style the `lb_popup` element:

```
#lb_popup
{
    color:#3366FF;
    width:250px;
    border:2px solid #0088CC;
    background:#fdfdfd;
    padding:4px 4px;
    display:none;
    position:absolute;
}
```

3. Edit our JavaScript `wp-live-blogroll.js` to position the pop up at mouse coordinates:

```
// create a new div and display a tip inside
$(this).append('<div id="lb_popup">' +
this.tip + '</div>');
// get coordinates
var mouseX = e.pageX || (e.clientX ? e.clientX
+ document.body.scrollLeft: 0);
var mouseY = e.pageY || (e.clientY ? e.clientY
+ document.body.scrollTop: 0);
// move the top left corner to the left and down
mouseX -= 260;
mouseY += 5;
// position our div
$('#lb_popup').
css({
    left: mouseX + "px",
    top: mouseY + "px"
    });
    // show it using a fadeIn function
    $('#lb_popup').fadeIn(300);
```

4. Finally, load the CSS style by using the `wp_head` action. Edit the `wp-live-blogroll.php` file and add this code to the end:

```
add_action('wp_head', 'WPLiveRoll_HeadAction' );
function WPLiveRoll_HeadAction()
{
  global $wp_live_blogroll_plugin_url;
  echo '<link rel="stylesheet"
  href="'.$wp_live_blogroll_plugin_url.'/wp-live-blogroll.css"
  type="text/css" />';
}
```

5. Be sure to upload all new files to the server. Once you reload the page you should get a newly created pop-up window just below the mouse pointer, that looks like this:

What just happened?

We created a pop-up window by applying CSS styling to it and placed it according to the current mouse position.

Our stylesheet is loaded using the `wp_head` (for admin pages wp_admin_head) action executed inside the `<head>` tag of the page:

```
add_action('wp_head', 'WPLiveRoll_HeadAction' );
function WPLiveRoll_HeadAction()
{
  global $wp_live_blogroll_plugin_url;
  echo '<link rel="stylesheet"
  href="'.$wp_live_blogroll_plugin_url.'/wp-live-blogroll.css"
  type="text/css" />';
}
```

In the CSS file we use '#' to reference our identifier (`<div id='lb_popup'>`). If we were referencing a class (possibly multiple elements) we would use a '.' instead):

```
#lb_popup
{
    color:#3366FF;
    width:250px;
    border:2px solid #0088CC;
    background:#fdfdfd;
    padding:4px 4px;
    display:none;
    position:absolute;
}
```

The style specifies several attributes including the width, font color and background color. We set the position to absolute as we will tell it exactly where to appear with the JavaScript. We also want to show the pop up using jQuery fade-in effect, so we set display to none as a default value.

The next snippet of code calculates the position of the mouse on our page:

```
// get coordinates
var mouseX = e.pageX || (e.clientX ? e.clientX
+ document.body.scrollLeft: 0);
var mouseY = e.pageY || (e.clientY ? e.clientY
+ document.body.scrollTop: 0);
```

We then offset the coordinates by a predefined amount to get the final desired position:

```
// move the top left corner to the left and down
mouseX -= 260;
mouseY += 5;
```

jQuery offers various functions for displaying hidden elements such as show, slide, animate and fadeIn.

In our example, we use the `fadeIn` effect with the optional parameter of fade-in speed in milliseconds:

```
// show it using a fadeIn function
$('#lb_popup).fadeIn(300);
```

Having solved the pop up, it's finally time to use Ajax. Lots of people still avoid using Ajax as the technology is still new. But we will show how to use it in a very simple manner.

Demystifying Ajax

Ajax is a technology that allows web pages to dynamically perform actions or updates. This allows for a higher level of user interactivity that we can see in popular applications such as Google Maps or Gmail.

Since its introduction in 2005, Ajax has stood out as an excellent addition to the web developer's arsenal, but several developers have been reluctant to use it due to certain initial problems and cross-browser compatibility issues.

Fortunately, today these issues are gone thanks to high-level libraries such as jQuery that take care of all Ajax calls internally and give us a simple to use API.

Simple example of using Ajax

Now that we have a pop up in place, we need to fill it with data from the RSS feeds. We have already learned how to parse RSS so all we have to do is create a function to display several posts from a feed at once, and fill our pop up with this information using Ajax.

Time for action – Use Ajax to dynamically retrieve feed posts

In order to work, Ajax usually needs to call a file on our server. This file is responsible for providing the response, and it is best that we put this Ajax functionality into a separate file.

1. Create a file called `wp-live-blogroll-ajax.php`, implying that we want to use it for handling Ajax requests.

2. Add the code to include the necessary files, read the URL parameter passed to the script and call our function to deal with the URL:

```php
<?php
/*
WP Live Blogroll Ajax script
Part of a WP Live Blog Roll plugin
*/
require_once("../../../wp-config.php");
require_once(ABSPATH . WPINC . '/rss.php');

// fetch information from GET method
$link_url = $_GET['link_url'];

// return the result
WPLiveRoll_Handle ajax($link_url);
```

3. We will also need a utility function to get an excerpt from the text. We will use it to show only the first 20 words from the post:

```
function WPLiveRoll_GetExcerpt($text, $length = 20 )
{
    $text = strip_tags($text);
    $words = explode(' ', $text, $length + 1);
    if (count($words) > $length)
    {
        array_pop($words);
        array_push($words, '[...]');
        $text = implode(' ', $words);
    }
    return $text;
}
```

4. We are going to add a function to parse the feed now. The function is similar to the first function we used at the beginning of the chapter, but it parses a number of posts and returns them in a formatted HTML. This function will return the result of our Ajax request.

```
function WPLiveRoll_HandleAjax($link_url)
{
    // we will return final HTML code in this variable
    $result='';

    // number of posts we are showing
    $number = 5;

    $link_url=trailingslashit($link_url);
    // pick the rss feed based on the site
    if (strstr($link_url,"blogspot"))
    {
        // blogspot blog
        $feed_url=$link_url."feeds/posts/default/";
    }
    else if (strstr($link_url,"typepad"))
    {
        // typepad blog
        $feed_url=$link_url."atom.xml";
    }
    else
    {
        // own domain or wordpress blog
```

```php
        $feed_url=$link_url."feed/";
     }

    // use WordPress to fetch the RSS feed
    $feedfile = fetch_rss($feed_url);

    // check if we got valid response
    if (is_array($feedfile->items ) && !empty(
                        $feedfile->items ) )
    {
        // slice the number of items we need
        $feedfile->items = array_slice($feedfile->items,
                        0, $number);

        // create HTML out of posts
           $result.= '<ul>';
        foreach($feedfile->items as $item )
        {
            // fetch the information
            $item_title = $item['title'];
            $item_link = $item['link'];
            $item_description =
            WPLiveRoll_GetExcerpt($item['description']);

            // form result
            $result.= '<li><a class="lb_link"
            target="'.$link_target.'" href="'.$item_link.'"
            >'.$item_title.'</a><p class="lb_desc">'
            .$item_description.'</p></li>';
        }
        $result.= '</ul>';
    }
    else
    {
        // in case we were unable to parse the feed
        $result.= "No posts available.";
    }

    // return the HTML code
    die( $result );
}
?>
```

5. In order to use Ajax we need to pass the url to our plugin to JavaScript. We will use `wp_localize_script` function to do that:

```
function WPLiveRoll_ScriptsAction()
{
  global $wp_live_blogroll_plugin_url;

  if (!is_admin())
  {
    wp_enqueue_script('jquery');
    wp_enqueue_script('wp_live_roll_script',
    $wp_live_blogroll_plugin_url.'/wp-live-blogroll.js',
    array('jquery'));

    // pass parameters to JavaScript
    wp_localize_script('wp_live_roll_script', 'LiverollSettings',
    array('plugin_url' => $wp_live_blogroll_plugin_url));
  }
}
```

6. The moment has come. We will use simple Ajax request (`load`) to get a response from the script we have made. The response will be automatically loaded into our element as HTML content:

```
$('#lb_popup').css
({
    left: mouseX + "px",
    top: mouseY + "px"
});
// use load() method to make an Ajax request
$('#lb_popup').load(LiverollSettings.plugin_url +
'/wp-live-blogroll-ajax.php?link_url=' + this.href);

// show it using a fadeIn function
$('#lb_popup').fadeIn(300);
```

7. We will comment out the text from the previous examples, and remove it from the `<div>`:

```
// set the text we want to display
// this.tip="Recent posts from " + this.href + "
// will be displayed here...";

// create a new div and append it to the link
$(this).append('<div id="lb_popup"></div>');
```

8. We are ready to see the plugin in action. Let us upload all the files and test it. You should get a pop-up window showing five latest posts from the site:

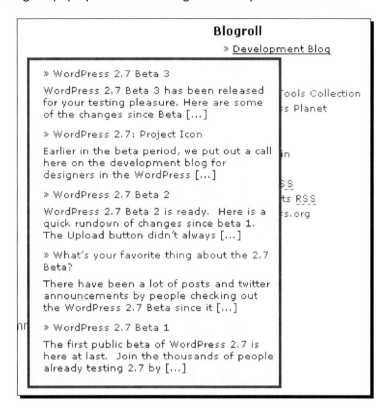

Congratulations! You have created a Live Blogroll plugin using jQuery and Ajax!

What just happened?

The main difference here over our previous examples is in the use of Ajax in our JavaScript.

We have used the jQuery `load()` function, which is the simplest way to call an external script and load the data into our page:

```
// use load() method to make an Ajax request
$('#lb_popup).load(LiverollSettings.plugin_url +
'/wp-live-blogroll-ajax.php?link_url=' + this.href);
```

Notice how we reference `lb_popup` when using the `load()` function. This will load any output of our script into the `lb_popup` element automatically.

Let's see now how our Ajax response script works.

First, we have created a new file `wp-live-blogroll-ajax.php` to handle our Ajax requests. At the beginning of the file we referenced these includes:

```
require_once("../../../wp-config.php");
require_once(ABSPATH . WPINC . '/rss.php');
```

Notice how we included `wp-config.php`. This is required because when our JavaScript calls the file, it will not be a part of WordPress code anymore, so we need to load all the WordPress functions and variables in order to use them. The easiest way is by including `wp-config.php`, which in turn includes all the other necessary WordPress files.

Locating `wp-config.php` like we did in our example is only a best guess at where the file is located and will work in most cases.

Since WordPress version 2.6, this file can be relocated anywhere in regards to plugin folder, so there is no certain way to tell its location. You are advised to check WordPress Codex for updated information on the topic.

Additionally, we included `rss.php` for `fetch_rss()` functionality.

Next, we read the link URL parameter that was passed to our file on the call from JavaScript. We use the GET method as the Ajax request was using that.

```
// fetch information from GET method
$link_url = $_GET['link_url'];
```

Next, we call the function for handling the feed:

```
// return the result
WPLiveRoll_HandleAjax($link_url);
```

This function uses an approach similar to the one we have already described. The difference begins with the feed processing part.

We want to process a number of posts (five by default); so we slice that number from the array of `feed` items:

```
// slice the number of items we need
$feedfile->items = array_slice($feedfile->items, 0, $number);
```

Next, we process each feed item and extract the title, link and description:

```
// create HTML out of posts
$result.= '<div><ul>';
foreach($feedfile->items as $item )
{
```

```
// fetch the information
$item_title = $item['title'];
$item_link = $item['link'];
$item_description =
WPLiveRoll_GetExcerpt($item['description']);
```

We prepare the code using a HTML list with this information:

```
// form result
$result.= '<li><a target="'.$link_target.'"
href="'.$item_link.'"
>'.$item_title.'</a><p>'.$item_description.'</p></li>';
```

In case we had a problem processing the feed, we will return a message:

```
    $result.= '</ul></div>';
}
else
{
    // in case we were unable to parse the feed
    $result.= "No posts available";
}
```

Finally, we return the result using the `die()` function to end our Ajax response script:

```
    // return the HTML code
    die( $result );
}
```

Using JavaScript with WordPress

The main difference between JavaScript and PHP is that JavaScript is client based (it executes in the user's browser) whereas PHP is server based (it executes on the remote server). This means JavaScript is good at handling user actions (clicking, moving the mouse, and so on) while PHP is good at dealing with server variables, database and other things happening remotely.

This also means that we need to find a way to connect the two. Most of the time, we need a way to pass variables from PHP to JavaScript and user actions from JavaScript to PHP.

Parsing parameters using wp_localize_script

WordPress provides `wp_localize_script` function which is an elegant way to pass the parameters to your JavaScript.

```
wp_localize_script('wp_live_roll_script', 'LiverollSettings',
array('plugin_url' => $wp_live_blogroll_plugin_url));
```

First parameter is our script's name followed by the name of JavaScript object that will hold the settings. Next you can specify the array of parameters.

These parameters will be available in JavaScript and can be accessed as
`LiverollSettings.plugin_url`

Ajax and WordPress

As we have seen, integrating Ajax functionality with WordPress is relatively easy. The basic Ajax flow chart looks generally like this:

1. The user does something on the page (like clicking or moving the mouse) and the JavaScript code is triggered. It then creates and calls another file on the server (Ajax response script).
2. Ajax response script will process the request based on our input parameters and return the output back to the browser.
3. The returned information is then processed and displayed by the JavaScript in the browser.

Ajax in admin panel

You can see examples of Ajax in the administration panel such as auto-saving of posts, moderating of comments or managing of your blogroll and categories.

For handling Ajax calls happening in the administration panel, there is another simple alternative.

The way this works is that we create a function for handling the Ajax request and assign it to the `wp_ajax` hook by extending it with the desired name, as shown here:

```
add_action('wp_ajax_my_function', 'my_function' );
```

Step two, we make an Ajax call to `admin-ajax.php` and send the name as a parameter. The jQuery call would look something like this:

```
$('#info').load('admin-ajax.php?action=my_function');
```

The most obvious benefit of this approach is that the Ajax handling function can freely be a part of your main script, and you can easily change it by assigning another function to the `wp_Ajax` action.

jQuery.ajax method

When we want more control, especially error handling, we will use the more advanced `Ajax()` function.

This function accepts several parameters of interest:

- ◆ `type`: The type of request to make ('POST' or 'GET'); the default is GET.
- ◆ `url`: The URL to be requested
- ◆ `timeout`: A set of local timeouts in miliseconds (ms) for the request
- ◆ `success`: A function to be called if the request succeeds
- ◆ `error`: A function to be called if the request fails
- ◆ `async`: By default, all requests are sent asynchronously. If you need synchronous requests, set this option to false. Synchronous requests may temporarily lock the browser, until the request is finished

Let's use this more advanced function in our JavaScript now.

Time for action – Use advanced Ajax call

In this example, we will replace the simple Ajax call with a more advanced one that offers us more options and controls.

Open the `wp-live-blogroll.js.php` file and replace the `load()` function with the `ajax()` function:

```
$.ajax
({
    type: "GET",
    url: LiverollSettings.plugin_url + '/wp-live-blogroll-ajax.php',
    timeout: 3000,
    data:
    {
      link_url: this.href
    },
    success: function(msg)
    {
```

```
        jQuery('#lb_popup').html(msg);
        jQuery('#lb_popup').fadeIn(300);
    },
    error: function(msg)
    {
        jQuery('#lb_popup').html('Error: ' + msg.responseText);
    }
})
```

What just happened?

We have used an advanced jQuery function for handling the Ajax request, which obviously offers us more parameters.

The function allows us to specify the request type ('POST' or 'GET'), maximum script timeout and handlers for success and error results. This gives us full control over the events.

 Full reference of the Ajax() function and available parameters are available at http://docs.jquery.com/Ajax/jQuery.Ajax

Ajax script security using nonces

WordPress provides a simple to use, but powerful security mechanism to protect your scripts from unauthorised execution by using the so called nonces.

Nonce means **number used once** and represents a unique number much like a password generated each time the script runs. The idea is to use nonces in order to verify whether our request was authentic.

Time for action – Add a security nonce

1. Open the wp-live-blogroll.js.php file and add create a nonce at the beginning of the script:

```
function WPLiveRoll_ScriptsAction()
{
    global $wp_live_blogroll_plugin_url;
    if (!is_admin())
    {
        // create a nonce
```

```
$nonce = wp_create_nonce('wp-live-blogroll');
wp_enqueue_script('jquery');
wp_enqueue_script('wp_live_roll_script',
$wp_live_blogroll_plugin_url.'/wp-live-blogroll.js',
array('jquery'));

   }
}
```

2. Modify the Ajax call to include the generated nonce as an additional parameter:

```
$.ajax
({
   type: "GET",
   url: LiverollSettings.plugin_url + '/wp-live-blogroll-ajax.php',
   timeout: 3000,
   data:
   {
      link_url: this.href,
      _ajax_nonce: '<?php echo $nonce; ?>'
   },
   success: function(msg)
   {
```

3. Modify `wp-live-blogroll-ajax.php` and add this check at the beginning of Ajax handler function:

```
function WPLiveRoll_Handle ajax($link_url)
{
    // check security
    check_ajax_referer( "wp-live-blogroll" );
```

With this simple modification, we have made sure that our Ajax handling script is used only when our plugin calls it.

What just happened?

When our script is run the next time, a unique nonce is created using the `wp_create_nonce()` function. We use a nonce identifier as a parameter:

```
$nonce = wp_create_nonce( 'wp-live-blogroll' );
```

We then pass this nonce as the `Ajax_nonce` parameter. WordPress checks this parameter automatically in the `check_ajax_referer` function, which also uses the nonce identifier parameter:

```
check_ajax_referer( "wp-live-blogroll" );
```

If the check fails, the script will simply exit at that point (internally, `die(-1)` happens).

Quick reference

`wp_create_nonce(nonce_id)`: It creates a unique nonce using the identifier.

`check_ajax_referer(nonce_id)`: It is used to check Ajax nonces; passed as the `ajax_nonce` parameter, using the nonce identifier.

To read more about possible security implication and Cross-Site Request Forgery (CSRF), visit `http://en.wikipedia.org/wiki/Cross-site_request_forgery`.

Summary

We have come a long way from the initial concept to the final plugin. We have learned that using jQuery and Ajax with WordPress does not have to be hard.

The **Live Blogroll** plugin we created made our blogroll more attractive and interactive. When the user hovers the mouse over the links, a list of recent posts is displayed using Ajax to retrieve the information. We learned how to use Ajax with high-level jQuery functions and easily process the retrieved data.

Specifically, we covered:

- **Blogroll**: Accessing and modifying information using WordPress filters hook
- **Fetching RSS feeds**: Using built-in WordPress functionality with caching
- **Use scripts and other code in <head> section:** Including JavaScript and CSS files using WordPress action hooks
- **Using jQuery**: Setting up a jQuery file, with its powerful set of functions, and using it later with Ajax support
- **Ajax**: Integrating Ajax with our scripts, and using it to generate content dynamically
- **Using nonces**: Securing your WordPress plugins using nonces

Both jQuery and Ajax offer huge possibilities for plugin development. Making your plugins interact more with the users is definitely a trend to follow in the future.

The next step in our journey through WordPress plugin development will be a cool, Ajax-powered, Wall widget allowing users to leave comments much like a shoutbox.

4
The Wall

As you may have noticeed, this chapter carries the name of a famous album, which rocked the music world back in 1982. The artists used an unusual mix of music and film to produce an exceptional piece of art.

In this chapter, we will be using the same mixed approach, by taking advantage of creative WordPress and JavaScript techniques, in order to create an Ajax powered 'Wall' for your blog's sidebar.

We will be relying on what we have learned so far—WordPress hooks, API calls, and jQuery. We will also introduce a way to use built-in WordPress functionalities to achieve our project goals—saving both effort and time.

This chapter will introduce quite a few interesting techniques such as:

- Creating a special type of plugin—the **Widget**
- Storing the wall comments in the database—working with **WordPress database**
- Enter data in the form and updating the wall dynamically—**Ajax form submit**

You will learn these techniques by:

- Creating the **Wall** widget that appears in your blog's side bar. Users can add a quick comment and it will appear in the sidebar immediately (without reloading the page).

The wall will increase the usability of any blog by presenting a global meeting place for all users to communicate.

The main concepts behind the Wall plugin

Before we start with our plugin, let's take a moment and create a design outline covering the main areas of the plugin.

- **Widget**: Obviously, the first thing on our list is to create a sidebar area for the wall. We will use WordPress widget API to do that.

- **Wall Comments**: We will store the user comments in the WordPress database.

- **Comment Management**: The administrator needs to be able to access comments, and approve, disapprove, or delete them.

- **Security and Spam protection**: Being on the front page and on most other pages of our site, the wall is exposed to various threats. We need to think of a way to protect our blog from unwanted spam.

- **Options and Styling**: Last but not least, we want to be able to customize the look of the widget. Since the wall will be constrained within a relatively small area (the sidebar), we need to carefully plan the look and the functionality of the widget.

The main development concerns here are the management of comments, and spam protection.

A typical PHP approach to address these concerns would be:

1. Create a database to store the comments in.

2. Create an administrative backend with comment management functionality.

3. Implement a set of rules for combating spam, such as black lists, user IP bans, and so on.

It is obvious that this approach needs a long development time. On the other hand, this is a book about WordPress, which is arguably the best blogging platform in the world today. Blogging includes a lot of commenting, and WordPress already features one of the most advanced commenting engines available. So why just not take advantage of it?

The main principle behind our idea is to dedicate a WordPress page as a place holder for all user comments. This allows us to use the WordPress commenting engine to take care of most of the hard work, such as adding the comments, administrative management and best of all—spam protection.

WordPress already comes with built-in comment spam and flood protection.

Discussion Settings

Default article settings

☐ Attempt to notify any blogs linked to from the article (slows down posting.)
☑ Allow link notifications from other blogs (pingbacks and trackbacks.)
☑ Allow people to post comments on the article
(These settings may be overridden for individual articles.)

E-mail me whenever

☑ Anyone posts a comment
☐ A comment is held for moderation

Before a comment appears

☐ An administrator must always approve the comment
☑ Comment author must fill out name and e-mail
☐ Comment author must have a previously approved comment

Comment Moderation

Hold a comment in the queue if it contains 2 or more links. (A common characteristic of comment spam is a large number of hyperlinks.)

When a comment contains any of these words in its content, name, URL, e-mail, or IP, it will be held in the moderation queue. One word or IP per line. It will match inside words, so "press" will match "WordPress".

Comment Blacklist

When a comment contains any of these words in its content, name, URL, e-mail, or IP, it will be marked as spam. One word or IP per line. It will match inside words, so "press" will match "WordPress".

There are also a number of popular anti-spam plugins such as Akismet that deal with the problem of spam in the comments. So instead of reinventing the wheel, we will leave these dedicated plugins to do the job.

By using built-in WordPress functionalities whenever we can, we also provide the opportunity for the plugin to develop itself automatically with the development of WordPress. For example, if the next version of WordPress brings comment editing in a super cool 3D way, all comments for our widget will become editable in the same way automatically.

This will allow us to spend more time focusing on other areas of the widget—like deciding which jQuery effects we can use to make it more attractive.

Use built-in WordPress functionalities whenever you can. Try to think outside of the box and find features of WordPress that can help you with your plugin. Always try to find fresh ways to re-use the code that a large community of WordPress developers has already contributed. It saves time and gets you free upgrades.

Creating a widget

Creating widgets is a simple three step process.

1. Create a function that will display the widget content.
2. Register that function as a widget using WordPress API.
3. Done! To enable the widget you need to activate it now in the administration panel.

Let's start our widget by displaying the 'Hello World!' text in the sidebar.

Time for action – Create a 'Hello World!' widget

As usual, we will start building our plugin with the necessary plugin information.

Later, we will create a function to display Hello World text and then register that function as a widget.

1. Create a new folder called `wp-wall`.

2. Create a new `wp-wall.php` file. Insert the following plugin information:

```
/*
Plugin Name: WP Wall
Version: 0.1
Description: "Wall" widget that appears in your blog's side bar
 Users can add a quick comment and it will appear in the
 sidebar immediately (without reloading the page).
Author: Vladimir Prelovac
Author URI: http://www.prelovac.com/vladimir
Plugin URI: http://www.prelovac.com/vladimir/
wordpress-plugins/wp-wall
*/

global $wp_version;

$exit_msg='WP Wall requires WordPress 2.6 or newer.
<a href="http://codex.wordpress.org/Upgrading_WordPress">Please
update!</a>';
```

```
if (version_compare($wp_version,"2.3","<"))
{
    exit ($exit_msg);
}
```

3. Add a variable that will hold the path to our plugin. We will use it later.

```
$wp_wall_plugin_url = trailingslashit( WP_PLUGIN_URL.'/'.
dirname( plugin_basename(__FILE__) );
```

4. Add the function for displaying the text:

```
function WPWall_Widget()
{
    echo "Hello World!";

}
```

5. Register our function as a widget. We do this by hooking to `init` action and using `register_sidebar_widget` call:

```
function WPWall_Init()
{
    // register widget
    register_sidebar_widget('WP Wall', 'WPWall_Widget');
}

add_action('init', 'WPWall_Init');

?>
```

6. Now upload and enable our plugin. Our widget will appear on the widgets page of the administrative panel. In order to make it active, you need to drag and drop it onto the sidebar.

7. Visit your site and you will notice the **Hello World!** text printed on your sidebar. I know it is not pretty yet, but we just wanted to get it out there for now.

What just happened?

The action hook `init` executes just after WordPress has finished loading. It is a good choice for inserting general plugin initialization code such as registering widgets. We use it to insert our `init` function:

```
add_action('init', 'WPWall_Init');
```

The widget is registered in WordPress with `register_sidebar_widget()` taking the widget name and the callback function responsible for drawing the widget.

```
function WPWall_Init()
{
    // register widget
    register_sidebar_widget('WP Wall', 'WPWall_Widget');
}
```

In our case, the callback function simply prints out the **Hello World!** text on the screen.

```
function WPWall_Widget()
{
    echo "Hello World!";
}
```

Register widgets with description

The official WordPress documentation encourages the use of the `register_sidebar_widget()` function for compatibility reasons, instead of the more powerful `wp_register_sidebar_widget()`.

The latter function allows us to enter the widget description, shown on the widgets screen.

Alternatively, you can use this code to register widget:

```
$widget_optionss = array('classname' => 'WPWall_Widget',
'description' => "A comments 'Wall' for your sidebar." );

wp_register_sidebar_widget('WPWall_Widget', 'WP Wall',
'WPWall_Widget', $widget_options);
```

Which shows a description for the widget:

Text	Add	Arbitrary text or HTML
RSS	Add	Entries from any RSS or Atom feed
Recent Comments	Add	The most recent comments
WP Wall	Add	A comments 'Wall' for your sidebar.

Quick reference

`Init`: Action best used for initializing plugin data ad registering widgets.

`register_sidebar_widget($name, $callback)`: Registers a widget with a name and a callback function parameter. More information is available at: `http://automattic.com/code/widgets/plugins/`

`wp_register_sidebar_widget($id, $name, $callback, $options)`: A more powerful way to register widgets allowing us to specify the description in the options.

Widget controls

Widgets have a control panel that can be changed, for example, to add options for the widget.

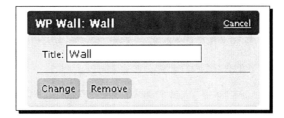

WordPress also provides a mechanism to make your widget compatible with various themes. It does this by passing several parameters to your widget's callback function. These parameters include the necessary tags and CSS classes which we need to include in order not to 'break' the theme.

Time for action – Expanding the widget with controls

In this example, we will expand our widget by adding additional widget features available to us through WordPress.

We will also learn how to read and save plugin options using WordPress.

1. Add the function to handle our widget control panel. It will parse the submitted data, save the title and print out the form:

```
function WPWall_WidgetControl()
{
    // get saved options
    $options = get_option('wp_wall');

    // handle user input
    if ( $_POST["wall_submit"] )
    {
        $options['wall_title'] = strip_tags( stripslashes(
        $_POST["wall_title"] ) );
        update_option('wp_wall', $options);
    }
    $title = $options['wall_title'];

    // print out the widget control
    include('wp-wall-widget-control.php');
}
```

2. Change our init function to register the widget control panel:

```
function WPWall_Init()
{
    // register widget
    register_sidebar_widget('WP Wall', 'WPWall_Widget');

    // register widget control
    register_widget_control('WP Wall', 'WPWall_WidgetControl');
}
```

3. Create the file, `wp-wall-widget-control.php`. This file will contain the HTML code of the control panel, and we can then simply `include()` it in our code. It is easier to edit and maintain the files this way. Here are the contents of our form:

```
<p>
<label for="wall_title">Title: <input  name="wall_title"
    type="text" value="<?php echo $title; ?>" /></label>

<input type="hidden" id="wall_submit" name="wall_submit"
                                       value="1" />
</p>
```

4. Edit the `WPWall_Widget()` function to output the title and theme compatibility code:

```
function WPWall_Widget($args = array())
{
    // extract the parameters
    extract($args);

    // get our options
    $options=get_option('wp_wall');
    $title=$options['wall_title'];

    // print the theme compatibility code
    echo $before_widget;
    echo $before_title . $title. $after_title;

    // include our widget
    include('wp-wall-widget.php');

    echo $after_widget;
}
```

5. Similarly, create `wp-wall-widget.php` and move the **Hello World!** there.

```
<p>Hello World!</p>
```

6. Upload all the new files and visit the **Widgets** panel.

You can see that our widget has gained an input form where you can type in the title and then click on the **Save Changes** button, to save the changes.

7. The changes are also immediately visible on our sidebar:

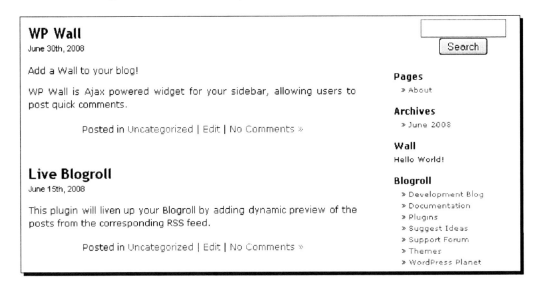

What just happened?

By registering the widget control panel, we gained the ability to show and save the settings relevant to our widget.

To register a widget control, simply call `register_widget_control()` with the name of the callback function that will handle the control panel:

```
// register widget control
register_widget_control('WP Wall', 'WPWall_WidgetControl');
```

The function can also accept two additional optional parameters–the desired width and height of the control. But you can safely leave them at the default settings.

WordPress options

Let's see how we use WordPress to store our plugin options.

WordPress provides two easy-to-use functions to handle plugin and widget options: `get_option()` to retrieve the options and `update_option()` to save them into the database.

Both accept the option name parameter—a unique identifier used to identify your option in the WordPress database. It is important to use a unique option name so that your option does not conflict with other plugins.

Use `get_option()` to retrieve the options:

```
$options = get_option('wp_wall');
```

Use `update_option()` to save the options. The `$options` variable is very flexible; for example, it can be either an object or an array:

```
// $options can be a string - or an array
update_option('wp_wall', $options);
```

We will cover options again in more detail when we cover the creation of your plugin options page later in the book.

Display widget control

We created `wp-wall-widget-control.php`, an external file to store our widget panel. It contains the title input field:

```
<label for="wall_title">Title: <input  name="wall_title"
type="text"
 value="<?php echo $title; ?>" /></label>
<input type="hidden" id="wall_submit" name="wall_submit" value="1"
/>
```

Our `WPWall_WidgetControl()` function retrieves the saved title and prints the form:

```
function WPWall_WidgetControl()
{
    // get saved options
    $options = get_option('wp_wall');

    $title = $options['wall_title'];

    // print out the widget control
    include('wp-wall-widget-control.php');
}
```

Handling widget input

When the user submits the form, the widget control function is called again, and we can use it to parse the submitted data.

We can check for submit action by inspecting the $_POST["wall_submit"], and then proceed to extract the title from `wall_title` field to store it in the database:

```
function WPWall_WidgetControl()
{
    // get saved options
    $options = get_option('wp_wall');

    // handle user input
    if ( $_POST["wall_submit"] )
    {
        $options['wall_title'] = strip_tags( stripslashes
        ($_POST["wall_title"]));

        update_option('wp_wall', $options);
    }
    $title = $options['wall_title'];

    // print out the widget control
    include('wp-wall-widget-control.php');
}
```

We use `strip_tags` and `stripslashes` to remove HTML and any other malformed code the user may enter.

Handling widget output

Now we need to show the widget on the sidebar. In order to achieve theme compatibility, we will display special parameters sent to our widget.

So first, we will extract the parameters:

```
function WPWall_Widget($args = array())
{
    // extract the parameters
    extract($args);
```

The most important ones are `before_widget, before_title, after_title,` and `after_widget` which contains the code we need to print out.

```
function WPWall_Widget($args)
{
    // extract the parameters
    extract($args);

    // get our options
    $options=get_option('wp_wall');
    $title=$options['wall_title'];

    // print the theme compatibility code
    echo $before_widget;
    echo $before_title . $title. $after_title;

    // include our widget
    include('wp-wall-widget.php');

    echo $after_widget;
}
```

The widget file currently just displays our **Hello World!**message.

```
<p>Hello World!</p>
```

For users of non-widgetized themes

For those users of your widget who do not have widget-enabled themes, it is advisable to provide instructions in your `readme.txt` file on how to use the plugin.

This usually includes instructions to call the widget output function (in our case `WPWall_Widget()`) directly from somewhere within the user's theme sidebar template.

Quick reference

`get_option($key)`: Retrieves the option specified by the key name. If the option does not exist, it returns FALSE. More information can be found at: `http://codex.wordpress.org/Function_Reference/get_option`

`update_option($key, $value)`: Saves the option value associated with a key. More information can be found at: `http://codex.wordpress.org/Function_Reference/update_option`

`register_widget_control($name, $callback, $width, $height)`: Registers a widget control in the administration panel. The function accepts the name of the control, the callback function to process information and optional width and height parameters. More information can be found at: `http://automattic.com/code/widgets/plugins/`

Create a WordPress page from the code

Now that we have covered everything we need regarding the widget, the next thing on our list is creating a WordPress page, which will be a placeholder for our wall comments.

WordPress comments do not specifically need to be assigned to a post or page; they can exist on their own. However, having them assigned to a page makes it easier to follow them. Moreover, should you decide to remove all the comments at once, you would only need to delete that page.

Time for action – Insert a page

We want to create the page at WordPress initialization. So we will use the init action just as we used it earlier.

We also want to be able to check if the page has already been created, so we will save the page ID in the options.

1. Let's start with modifying the init function to include page check and create code:

```
function WPWall_Init()
{
    // register widget
    register_sidebar_widget('WP Wall', 'WPWall_Widget');
    // register widget control
    register_widget_control('WP Wall', 'WPWall_WidgetControl');

    $options = get_option('wp_wall');

    // get our wall pageId
```

```
    $pageId=$options['pageId'];

    // check if the actual post exists
    $actual_post=get_post($pageId);

    // check if the page is already created
    if (!$pageId || !$actual_post ||
    ($pageId!=$actual_post->ID))
    {
        // create the page and save it's ID
        $options['pageId'] = WPWall_CreatePage();

        update_option('wp_wall', $options);
    }
}
```

2. Next, we want to create a function for inserting a page into the WordPress database

```
function WPWall_CreatePage()
{
    // create post object
    class mypost
    {
        var $post_title;
        var $post_content;
        var $post_status;
        var $post_type; // can be 'page' or 'post'
        var $comment_status; // open or closed for commenting
    }

    // initialize the post object
    $mypost = new mypost();

    // fill it with data
    $mypost->post_title = 'WP Wall Guestbook';
    $mypost->post_content = 'Welcome to my WP Wall Guestbook!';
    $mypost->post_status = 'draft';
    $mypost->post_type = 'page';
    $mypost->comment_status = 'open';

    // insert the post and return it's ID
    return wp_insert_post($mypost);
}
```

3. The next time WordPress loads, a new page will be created:

We've got a placeholder page for our Wall!

What just happened?

The code that we inserted into the init, so that the function executes with the next WordPress reload, does a couple of things. First, it checks if there is an already created page by retrieving the saved page ID from the options.

```
$options = get_option('wp_wall');
// get our wall pageId
$pageId=$options['pageId'];
```

Next, it tries to get a WordPress post associated with this ID. This way, we can check if the page still exists (the user could have accidently deleted it).

We are using the get_post() function, which returns a post object taking an ID as a parameter:

```
// check if the actual post exists
$actual_post=get_post($pageId);
```

If the page does not exist, we will create it and save the ID in the options:

```
// check if the page is already created
if (!$pageId || !$actual_post || ($pageId!=$actual_post->ID) )
{
    // create the page and save it's ID
    $options['pageId']=    WPWall_CreatePage();
    update_option('wp_wall', $options);
}
```

Let's take a look now at `WPWall_CreatePage()` which handles page creation.

In order to insert a post into the WordPress database, we need to specify relevant post information. An elegant way to do this is to create a post object:

```
function WPWall_CreatePage()
{
    // create post object
    class mypost
    {
        var $post_title;
        var $post_content;
        var $post_status;   // draft, published
        var $post_type;     // can be 'page' or 'post'
        var $comment_status; // open or closed for commenting
    }
    // initialize the post object
    $mypost = new mypost();
```

Next, we fill the variables. We will give our post a distinguishable title so that users can find it easily.

We also want to set the status of the page to **Draft** instead of **Published**– as we do not want this page to appear on the site at this moment:

```
    // fill it with data
    $mypost->post_title = 'WP Wall';
    $mypost->post_content =  "This is a placeholder page for your
    WP Wall. Do not delete or publish this page.";
    $mypost->post_status = 'draft';
    $mypost->post_type = 'page';
    $mypost->comment_status = 'open';
```

Finally, we want to insert the post into the WordPress database by using `wp_insert_post()`. It will return an ID of the post, which we will save for later use.

```
        // insert the post and return it's ID
        return wp_insert_post($mypost);
}
```

This completes the process of inserting a post into the database.

Quick reference

`get_post($id, $output)`: Takes the post ID and returns the database record for that post. Data can be in any of the various formats specified by the optional output parameter, and defaults to object. If the post does not exist, it returns `null`. More information can be found at: `http://codex.wordpress.org/Function_Reference/get_post`

`wp_insert_post($post)`: Function to insert posts and pages to WordPress database. Post can be an object or array containing information about the post such as `post_title`, `post_content`, `post_type`, and so on. Returns the ID of the post on success; otherwise returns 0. More information can be found at: `http://codex.wordpress.org/Function_Reference/wp_insert_post`

Handling user input

We have sorted out where to keep the user comments, so now we can move onto the comment form and user input.

Since we already have our widget set up, the next step will just involve editing the `wp-wall-widget.php` file and inserting the HTML for the form.

We want the form to have two fields: one for the name and the other for the comment text. Users who are logged-in will be recognized, and their name will be filled-in automatically.

Time for action – Create the wall comment form

To create our form, we will simply edit the HTML of our widget file.

1. Edit the `wp-wall-widget.php` file and replace the 'Hello World!' code with the following code:

```
<div id="wp_wall">

  <div id="wall_post">
    <form action="#" method="post" id="wallform">

      <?php if ( $user_ID ) : ?>

      <p>Logged in as <a href="<?php echo
      get_bloginfo('wpurl'); ?>/wp-admin/profile.php">
      <?php echo $user_identity; ?></a>.</p>

      <?php else : ?>

      <p>
      <label for="author"><small>Name</small></label><br/>
```

```
<input type="text" name="author" id="author" value=""
 tabindex="1"  />
</p>

<?php endif; ?>

<p>
<label for="comment"><small>Comment</small></label><br/>
<textarea name="comment" id="comment" rows="3"
 tabindex="2"></textarea>
</p>

<p><input name="submit_wall_post" type="submit"
 id="submit_wall_post" tabindex="3" value="Submit" /></p>
</form>
</div>
</div>
```

2. The form we created uses the global variables $user_ID and $user_identity to check if the user is logged in. We will reference them in the WPWall_Widget() function:

```
function WPWall_Widget($args)
{
    global  $user_ID,  $user_identity;

    // extract the parameters
    extract($args);
```

3. Let's also add CSS to our form to spice it up. Create the file, wp-wall.css:

```
#wp_wall p
{
    margin-top:4px;
    margin-bottom:4px;
}

#wallcomments p
{
    margin-top:5px;
    margin-bottom:5px;
}

#wall_post input
{
    border: 1px solid #cccccc;
}
```

4. We need to make sure our CSS loads by adding the code for the `wp_head` action at the end of the `wp-wall.php` file:

```
add_action('wp_head', 'WPWall_HeadAction' );

function WPWall_HeadAction()
{
    global $wp_wall_plugin_url;
    echo '<link rel="stylesheet" href="'.$wp_wall_plugin_url.'
    /wp-wall.css" type="text/css" />';
}
```

5. And the final result will look like this:

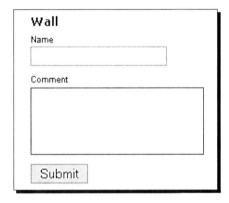

6. When the admin user is logged in, it will look like this:

Soon, we will be able to actually process the submitted content and display it.

What just happened?

Our widget now shows an HTML form with the name and comment area.

```
<div id="wall_post">
  <form action="#" method="post" id="wallform">
    <p>
      <label for="author"><small>Name</small></label><br/>
      <input type="text" name="author" id="author" value=""
       tabindex="1" />
    </p>
    <p>
      <label for="comment"><small>Comment</small></label><br/>
      <textarea name="comment" id="comment" rows="3"
       tabindex="2"></textarea>
    </p>
    <p>
      <input name="submit_wall_post" type="submit"
       id="submit_wall_post" tabindex="3" value="Submit" />
    </p>
  </form>
</div>
```

We also added a check to see if the current user is logged in.

In order to do that, we referenced the global variables `$user_ID` and `$user_identity`. Those variables provided by WordPress hold the ID of the currently logged in user with a matching user name:

```
global  $user_ID, $user_identity;
```

If the `user_ID` variable contains a valid ID, it means the user is logged in. In that case, we can print the logged-in user's details.

```
<form action="#" method="post" id="wallform">
  <?php if ( $user_ID ) : ?>
    <p>Logged in as <a href="<?php echo
      get_bloginfo('wpurl'); ?>/wp-admin/profile.php">
  <?php echo $user_identity; ?></a>.</p>
```

Otherwise, just print the input field for the name:

```
<?php else : ?>
  <p>
    <label for="author"><small>Name</small></label><br/>
    <input type="text" name="author" id="author" value=""
     tabindex="1"  />
```

```
    </p>
<?php endif; ?>
  <p>
    <label for="comment"><small>Comment</small></label><br/>
    <textarea name="comment" id="comment" rows="3"
     tabindex="2"></textarea>
  </p>
```

We load the CSS file using the wp_head action, which we also used in the previous chapter. It allows us to insert scripts and CSS style references directly into the <head> of the document:

```
add_action('wp_head', 'WPWall_HeadAction' );
function WPWall_HeadAction()
{
    global $wp_wall_plugin_url;
    echo '<link rel="stylesheet" href="'.$wp_wall_plugin_url.'/
    wp-wall.css" type="text/css" />';
}
```

We have prepared for the actual handling of the comments. We have the widget and the form ready, so we are ready for our next task—handling submitted comments.

Managing Ajax comment submit

We will now expand our Ajax knowledge with Ajax submit form technique.

The principle remains the same. jQuery will respond to an event (in this case, a user submitting the form) and instead of reloading the page, it will call an external script and display the results.

Our script on the other end will receive form information, and after validation, insert the comment into the WordPress database.

Finally, we will show a status message to the user, letting them know that the comment has been accepted:

Time for action – Save the comments

In this example, we will learn how to handle submit forms using Ajax.

We will also learn how to save the comments in the WordPress database.

1. Create the `wp-wall-ajax.php` file which will handle submitted form through a series of simple checks:

```php
<?php

require_once("../../../wp-config.php");

if ($_POST['submit_wall_post'])
{
    $options = get_option('wp_wall');

    $comment_post_ID=$options['pageId'];
    $actual_post=get_post($comment_post_ID);

    // sanity check to see if our page exists
    if (!$comment_post_ID || !$actual_post ||
    ($comment_post_ID!=$actual_post->ID) )
    {
        wp_die('Sorry, there was a problem posting your comment.
        Please try again.');
    }

    // extract data we need
    $comment_author = trim(strip_tags($_POST['author']));
    $comment_content = trim($_POST['comment']);

    // If the user is logged in get his name
    $user = wp_get_current_user();
    if ( $user->ID )
        $comment_author  = $user->display_name;

    // check if the fields are filled
    if ( '' == $comment_author )
        wp_die('Error: please type a name.');

    if ( '' == $comment_content )
        wp_die('Error: please type a comment.');

    // insert the comment
    $commentdata = compact('comment_post_ID', 'comment_author',
     'comment_content', 'user_ID');

    $comment_id = wp_new_comment( $commentdata );

    // check if the comment is approved
    $comment = get_comment($comment_id);
```

```
        if ($comment->comment_approved==0)
            wp_die('Your comment is awaiting moderation.');
        // return status
        die ( 'OK' );
    }
    ?>
```

2. Now, create the `wp-wall.js` file to handle our jQuery and Ajax stuff:

```javascript
// setup everything when document is ready
jQuery(document).ready(function($) {

    $('#wallform').ajaxForm({

    // handler function for success event
    success: function(responseText, statusText)
    {

      $('#wallresponse').html('<span class="wall-success">
      '+'Thank you for your comment!'+'</span>');
    },

    // handler function for errors
    error: function(request) {

      // parse it for WordPress error
      if (request.responseText.search(/<title>WordPress
      &rsaquo; Error<\/title>/) != -1)
      {

        var data = request.responseText.match(/<p>(.*)<\/p>/);
        $('#wallresponse').html('<span class="wall-error">'+
        data[1] +'</span>');
      }
      else
      {

        $('#wallresponse').html('<span class="wall-error">An
        error occurred, please notify the
        administrator.</span>');
      }
    } ,
    beforeSubmit: function(formData, jqForm, options) {
      // clear response div
      $('#wallresponse').empty();
    }
  });
});
```

3. We now need to load our script, jQuery and jQuery-Form libraries. The latter is used for handling Ajax form submits.

Add this code at the end of `wp-wall.php`:

```
add_action('wp_print_scripts', 'WPWall_ScriptsAction');
function WPWall_ScriptsAction()
{
    global $wp_wall_plugin_url;

    wp_enqueue_script('jquery');
    wp_enqueue_script('jquery-form');
    wp_enqueue_script('wp_wall_script',$wp_wall_plugin_url.
     '/wp-wall.js', array('jquery', 'jquery-form')); }
```

4. Add the URL to our Ajax handler script to the form's action field in `wp-wall-widget.php`. This is the script that will be called when the user clicks on **Submit**.

```
<div id="wall_post">
    <form action="<?php echo $wp_wall_plugin_url.'/
    wp-wall-ajax.php'; ?>" method="post" id="wallform">

    <?php if ( $user_ID ) : ?>
```

5. Add a `<div>` for script responses at the end of the form. We will use it to show status messages:

```
        <p><input name="submit_wall_post" type="submit"
         id="submit_wall_post" tabindex="3" value="Submit" /></p>

    </form>
</div>
        <div id="wallresponse"></div>
</div>
```

6. Update all the files. You are now ready to post comments:

7. And if you go to the **Manage Comments** administration panel you can see our comments listed:

Congratulations! An important part of the plugin functionality has been achieved.

We can now add as many comments as we want and manage them through our WordPress administration panel.

What just happened?

When the user submits a form, normally the URL given in the form's action is called:

```
<form action="<?php echo $wp_wall_plugin_url.
  '/wp-wall-ajax.php'; ?>" method="post" id="wallform">
```

If we do not use jQuery Ajax to handle submissions, our browser will load `wp-wall-ajax.php` as a new page and show the output of the script.

However, jQuery form library allows us to assign form submissions to Ajax calls easily.

So we have loaded all the necessary libraries using the `wp_print_scripts` action hook:

```
add_action('wp_print_scripts', 'WPWall_ScriptsAction');
function WPWall_ScriptsAction()
{
    global $wp_wall_plugin_url;

    wp_enqueue_script('jquery');
    wp_enqueue_script('jquery-form');
    wp_enqueue_script('wp_wall_script', $wp_wall_plugin_url.'/
    wp-wall.js', array('jquery', 'jquery-form'));
}
```

Using Ajax to submit forms

The jQuery form module provides the `ajaxForm()` method, which can automatically handle form submits using Ajax. It hooks to necessary events (like the user pressing the **Submit** button), submits the form dynamically using an Ajax call and displays the results.

We use the `ajaxForm` method with `#wallform`, which is the ID of our form:

```
// setup everything when document is ready
jQuery(document).ready(function($)
{
    $('#wallform').ajaxForm
    ({
```

The `ajaxForm()` function provides three useful events we can use for extra configuration.

The first is `beforeSubmit`, which executes just before the form is submitted. It is usually used to process the fields or do some kind of form validation.

In our case, we will clear the response `<div>`.

```
    $('#wallform').ajaxForm
    ({
        beforeSubmit: function(formData, jqForm, options)
        {
            // clear response div
            $('#wallresponse').empty();
        }
    });
});
```

Next, we will hook up to the `error` event, which executes in the event of a script failure.

Since we are using `wp_die()` to exit our comment handling script, we need to parse the response:

```
// setup everything when document is ready
jQuery(document).ready(function($)
{

  $('#wallform').ajaxForm
  ({
    // handler function for errors
    error: function(request)
    {
      // parse it for WordPress error
      if (request.responseText.search(/<title>WordPress
      &rsaquo; Error<\/title>/) != -1) {
```

If the response is valid, we extract the error message and print it out in our `wallresponse` div:

```
// parse it for WordPress error
if (request.responseText.search(/<title>WordPress
&rsaquo; Error<\/title>/) != -1)
{
  var data = request.responseText.match(/<p>(.*)<\/p>/);
  $('#wallresponse').html('<span class="wall-error">'+
  data[1] +'</span>');
```

Since we are using WordPress comment handling, we can expect errors ranging from duplicate comments, comment flooding, protection, and so on. We get all this comment checking functionality for free.

In case of wrong or malformed error response, we will print out a default error message:

```
}
else
{
   $('#wallresponse').html('<span class="wall-error">
   An error occurred, please notify the
   administrator.</span>'); }
},
beforeSubmit: function(formData, jqForm, options)
{
   // clear response div
   $('#wallresponse').empty();
}
```

Finally, we will hook up to the `success` event, which will run when our comment is submitted successfully. If everything goes fine, we will print out a simple 'Thank you' message:

```
// setup everything when document is ready
jQuery(document).ready(function($)
{
    $('#wallform').ajaxForm({

    // handler function for success event
    success: function(responseText, statusText)
    {
       $('#wallresponse').html('<span class="wall-success">'+'Thank
       you for your comment!'+'</span>');
    },
    // handler function for errors
    error: function(request)
    {
```

Saving comments in WordPress post

Let's see how the submitted comments are parsed and saved by WordPress.

We check the $_POST variable first to confirm that a comment is being posted:

```
    if ($_POST['submit_wall_post'])
    {
```

Next, a sanity check is performed to see if everything is all right with our wall page that is used for saving the comments:

```
$options = get_option('wp_wall');

$comment_post_ID=$options['pageId'];
$actual_post=get_post($comment_post_ID);

// sanity check to see if our page exists
if (!$comment_post_ID || !$actual_post ||
($comment_post_ID!=$actual_post->ID) )
{
    wp_die('Sorry, there was a problem posting your comment.
    Please try again.');
}
```

We use `wp_die()` to exit from our script in case of an error, passing it the error message. This will also automatically cause the Ajax call to return an `error` status.

Next, we extract the comment fields from the `$_POST` variable:

```
// extract data we need
$comment_author = trim(strip_tags($_POST['author']));
$comment_content = trim($_POST['comment']);
```

If the user is logged in, we want to use his display name as the comment author's name.

To do this, we use `wp_get_current_user()`. It returns an object containing user information such as user ID and name.

```
// If the user is logged in get his name
$user = wp_get_current_user();
if ( $user->ID )
  $comment_author   = $user->display_name;
```

Now, we can proceed to insert the comment. First, we use `compact()` to fill the comment data into an array, passing it the variables we need. We insert the comment using the `wp_new_comment` function.

```
// insert the comment
$commentdata = compact('comment_post_ID', 'comment_author',
'comment_content', 'user_ID');

$comment_id = wp_new_comment( $commentdata );
```

After the comment is inserted, we check to see if it was approved or not. Some blog administrators like to keep all the comments for approval, in which case the comment will not show up immediately:

```
// check if the comment is approved
$comment = get_comment($comment_id);

if ($comment->comment_approved==0)
    wp_die('Your comment is awaiting moderation.');
```

Finally, if everything is ok, we use `die()` method to just exit the script. The parameter is optional in this case, as we are not showing it anywhere:

```
// return status
die ( 'OK' );
}
```

> **Quick reference**
>
>
>
> `ajaxForm(options)` (jQuery): Used to submit forms with Ajax. The options object has among others are the `success`, `error` and the `beforeSubmit` callback events. More information can be found at: `http://www.malsup.com/jquery/form/`
>
> `wp_get_current_user()`: Returns information about the current user in an object including ID, `display_name`, email, and so on. More information can be found at: `http://codex.wordpress.org/Function_Reference/get_currentuserinfo`
>
> `wp_new_comment($commentdata)`: Inserts a comment into the database accepting the comment data array; returns a comment ID.
>
> `get_comment($id)`: Takes a comment ID and returns comment information in an object. We used it to check the comment_approved field. More information can be found at: `http://codex.wordpress.org/Function_Reference/get_comment`
>
> `wp_die($message)`: Exits the script returning Internal server error 500 HTTP header and the specified error message.

Dynamically load comments

We are now ready to display the comments we entered on our wall. They are already saved in the WordPress database, so just we need to extract and show them on our widget.

We will also create a mechanism to reload the comments automatically when the user submits the form.

Time for action – Display the comments

1. Add a new function, `WPWall_ShowComments()` at the end of `wp-wall.php`:

```php
function WPWall_ShowComments()
{
    global $wpdb;

    // get our page id
    $options = get_option('wp_wall');
    $pageId=$options['pageId'];

    // number of comments to display
    $number=5;

    $result='';

    // get comments from WordPress database
    $comments = $wpdb->get_results
    ("SELECT *
      FROM $wpdb->comments
      WHERE comment_approved = '1' AND comment_post_ID=$pageId
      AND NOT (comment_type = 'pingback' OR comment_type =
      'trackback')
      ORDER BY comment_date_gmt DESC LIMIT $number
    ");
    if ( $comments )
    {
        // display comments one by one
        foreach ($comments as $comment)
        {
            $result.= '<p><span class="wallauthor">' .
            $comment->comment_author.'</span><span class="wallcomment">:
            '.$comment->comment_content.'</span></p>';
        }
    }
    return $result;
}
```

2. Add the code to display comments to our widget. Edit the **wp-wall-widget.php** file and add a 'wallcomments' div, inside which we will display our comments:

```html
<div id="wp_wall">

    <div id="wallcomments">
        <?php echo WPWall_ShowComments (); ?>
    </div>

    <div id="wall_post">
```

3. Add this CSS to the end of `wp-wall.css` to style our comments:

```
#wallcomments
{
    margin-bottom: 5px;
    /* uncomment this for fixed height and a scrollbar
    height: 200px;
    overflow: auto; */
}
.wallauthor
{
    font-weight:bold;
}
.wallcomment
{
    font-weight:normal;
}
```

Reload the page, and you can see the comments:

4. Let's also reload the comments when the user posts a new one.

We will use an `ajaxForm target` property to display the results from our script:

```
jQuery(document).ready(function($)
{
    $('#wallform').ajaxForm({
    // target identifies the element(s) to update with the server
    response
    target: '#wallcomments',
    // handler function for success event
    success: function(responseText, statusText)
    {
```

5. Modify `wp-wall-ajax.php` script so it returns the comments:

```
        if ($comment->comment_approved==0)
          wp_die('Your comment is awaiting moderation.');
        // return status
        die ( WPWall_ShowComments() );
      }
    }
    ?>
```

6. Our plugin is fully working now. The new comments now appear without the page reload.

Good job!

We got the plugin working exactly as we wanted.

What just happened?

Our new `WPWall_ShowComments()` function is responsible for showing the user comments. It does this by executing a WordPress database query to get the recent comments.

WordPress database query

The WordPress database queries are easy thanks to the `wpdb` WordPress class. It provides the interface for handling database manipulations. In this case, we will use the `get_results()` method to retrieve the rows from the database quickly.

First, we prepare the information for the query, such as `pageId` and the number of comments:

```
function WPWall_ShowComments()
{
    global $wpdb;

    // get our page id
    $options = get_option('wp_wall');
    $pageId=$options['pageId'];

    // number of comments to display
    $number=5;

    $result='';
```

Next, we need to prepare the query. Let's analyze it for a moment.

We want to `SELECT` all comments `FROM` the comments table referenced by `$wpdb->comments`. This is the comments table of WordPress.

Our function `WHERE` states that we need comments posted under our **Wall** page, and not of the `pingback` or `trackback` types, which are special types of comments.

At the end, we want to sort the comments by comment date in descending order (`DESC ORDER`), and `LIMIT` them to the last five.

Here is the actual query:

```
// get comments from WordPress database
$comments = $wpdb->get_results
("SELECT *
  FROM $wpdb->comments
  WHERE comment_approved = '1' AND comment_post_ID=$pageId
  AND NOT (comment_type = 'pingback' OR comment_type =
  'trackback')
  ORDER BY comment_date_gmt DESC
  LIMIT $number
 ");
```

Comment output

By dividing the author name and the actual comment into separate CSS classes, later, the user can control the display though the CSS file.

```
if ( $comments )
{
    // display comments one by one
```

```
        foreach ($comments as $comment)
        {
          $result.= '<p><span class="wallauthor">' . $comment-
          >comment_author.'</span><span class="wallcomment">:
          '.$comment->comment_content.'</span></p>';
        }
      }
    return $result;
  }
```

Displaying the comments

We use our new function to show the comments within a `wallcomments <div>` in our widget:

```
<div id="wallcomments">
        <?php echo WPWall_ShowComments (); ?>
</div>
```

Next, by using the `target` parameter of the `ajaxForm()` function, we can specify where we want the Ajax script response to be directed to. This allows us to fill in the `wallcomments <div>` with new information.

```
$('#wallform').ajaxForm
({
    // target identifies the element(s) to update with the
    server response
    target: '#wallcomments',
```

Finally, we needed to make sure that our script returns comments instead of just 'OK'.

```
    // return status
    die ( WPWall_ShowComments() );
```

We have now achieved our desired functionality. The comments are submitted with Ajax, and added to the database, while the last few are retrieved and shown on the page.

Quick function reference

`$wpdb`: WordPress database interface class. Use `$wpdb->get_results()` to get rows for a given query quickly. More information can be found at: `http://codex.wordpress.org/Function_Reference/wpdb_Class`

Ajax security

Finally, we want to add a layer of security to our plugin. We will use nonces similar to those in the Live Blogroll plugin.

Time for action – Display the comments

1. Edit the `wp-wall-widget.php` file and add a nonce to the form using `wp_nonce_field`:

```
<form action="<?php echo $wp_wall_plugin_url.'/wp-wall-ajax.php';
?>" method="post" id="wallform">

  <?php wp_nonce_field('wp-wall'); ?>
  <?php if ( $user_ID ) : ?>
```

2. Add the check for nonce in the `wp-wall-ajax.php` file:

```
if ($_POST['submit_wall_post'])
{
    // security check
    check_ajax_referer('wp-wall');
    $options = get_option('wp_wall');
```

What just happened?

Adding nonces is a sure way to secure our plugins against CSRF attacks.

We can use the `wp_nonce_field()` function to automatically generate a nonce in forms. You can then use `check_ajax_referer()` to check for nonce in the Ajax response script. The function will automatically abort the execution of the script if there is a security threat.

Have a go Hero

The plugin has a lot of potential for feature upgrades. Why don't you try adding a few?

- Add an RSS feed to the wall comments. WordPress already has RSS feeds for all the post comments; you only need to get the link (hint: use the `get_post_comments_feed_link` function).

- Implement more options for the widget such as the number of comments to be shown, and a checkbox to disable the addition of new comments.

- Use jQuery to add effects to the form such as fading in the comments.

- Add a **Refresh** option so that the wall updates itself automatically after a specified time period (you can use the `setInterval` function).

- Provide a link to display all the comments by showing the comments page (user has to publish it previously).

Summary

In this chapter, we have learned an important lesson, which is that by utilizing built-in WordPress functionalities whenever we can, we are able to save both time and effort. And our shared plugin functionality will automatically follow the development of WordPress.

The Ajax Wall widget allows you to post quick comments. The comments will of course need to pass all internal verifications of WordPress before they can appear on our page. And we can easily manage comments from the WordPress administration interface.

We have covered important areas of WordPress development:

- **Widgets**: Creating and managing widgets on our blog
- **Options**: Using WordPress to manage our plugin options easily
- **Database**: Working with WordPress database to insert and retrieve information
- **Ajax forms**: Submitting forms and get the results without reloading the page

In the next chapter, we are going to look over more WordPress features and development techniques by developing a super cool Snazzy Archives plugin.

5
Snazzy Archives

This chapter covers the creation of a very sleek and stylish looking WordPress enhancement. The purpose of the **Snazzy Archives** plugin will be to present your site archives in a unique visual way.

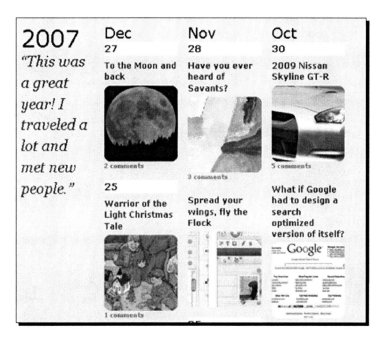

In order to achieve this visual output, we will read all posts from the WordPress database and display them using a combination of HTML, CSS, and jQuery.

We will incorporate our plugin into a PHP class to make it easier to use and maintain. We will also learn a few template tricks and how to integrate the plugin output to WordPress pages easily.

Finally, we will create an options page so that users can control various aspects of the plugin.

In summary, this chapter will teach you how to:

♦ Use a **PHP class** to describe your plugin

♦ Use **shortcode API** to display output on your pages, and use **custom templates** when you want more control

♦ **Manage options** for your plugin

♦ **Create options page** and **add administration menus**

♦ Create simple **caching mechanism** to speed up the output of your plugins

And you will learn this by creating a stylish **archive** view for your WordPress site.

Using a class for plugin

Let's start with learning a new way to code your plugins. We will use a PHP class, and add properties (variables) and methods (functions) to it.

Time for action – Create a new plugin class

Let's start building our plugin by creating our first class:

1. Create a new folder called `snazzy-archives`.

2. Create a new file, `snazzy-archives.php`:

```php
<?php
  /*
    Plugin Name: Snazzy Archives
    Version: 0.1
    Plugin URI: http://www.prelovac.com/vladimir/wordpress-plugins/
                snazzy-archives
    Author: Vladimir Prelovac
    Author URI: http://www.prelovac.com/vladimir
    Description: Express your blog through a unique representation
                of your post archives.
  */

  global $wp_version;

  $exit_msg = 'Snazzy Archives require WordPress 2.6 or newer.
               <a href="http://codex.wordpress.org/
               Upgrading_WordPress">Please update!</a>';
if (version_compare($wp_version, "2.6", "<"))
{
  exit($exit_msg);
```

3. Then add declaration for our class as follows:

```
// Avoid name collisions.
if ( !class_exists('SnazzyArchives') ) :

class SnazzyArchives
{
// this variable will hold url to the plugin
    var $plugin_url;

    // Initialize the plugin
    function SnazzyArchives()
    {

        $this->plugin_url = trailingslashit( WP_PLUGIN_URL.'/'.
         dirname( plugin_basename(__FILE__) ) );
    }

    // function to call after plugin activation
    function install()
    {

    }

}

else :

    exit ("Class SnazzyArchives already declared!");
endif;
```

4. Create an instance of our class:

```
// create new instance of the class
$SnazzyArchives = new SnazzyArchives();
```

5. And finally register the function we want to run when the plugin is activated:

```
if (isset($SnazzyArchives))
{
    // register the activation function by passing the reference
      to our instance
      register_activation_hook( __FILE__, array(&$SnazzyArchives,
      'install') );
}
?>
```

That's it! We have incorporated our plugin into an effective class in just a few steps.

What just happened?

Our plugin is now represented with a PHP class. The only name we need to worry about is the class name. So we want to use a unique name; same as the plugin name is probably a good idea.

Before the class is declared, we check its name using the PHP `class_exists()` function:

```
// Avoid name collisions.
if ( !class_exists('SnazzyArchives') ) :
```

In case of a name collision, we display an error message:

```
else :
    exit ("Class SnazzyArchives already declared!");
endif;
```

We can now declare variables and functions freely inside the class, without having to use long and unique prefixes to distinguish them.

First, we declare a variable that will hold our plugin URL:

```
class SnazzyArchives
{
    // this variable will hold url to the plugin
    var $plugin_url;
```

The class constructor function has the same name as the class, and executes whenever a new instance of the class is created.

We will use it to store initialization functions. For now, we will only fill the plugin URL into a variable:

```
class SnazzyArchives
{
    // this variable will hold url to the plugin
    var $plugin_url;
    // Initialize the plugin
    function SnazzyArchives()
    {
        $this->plugin_url=trailingslashit( get_bloginfo('wpurl') )
        .PLUGINDIR.'/'. dirname( plugin_basename(__FILE__) );
    }
```

Finally, we declare an empty function which we will use later to set the default options for the plugin.

```
function SnazzyArchives()
{
  $this->plugin_url=trailingslashit( get_bloginfo('wpurl') )
  .PLUGINDIR.'/'. dirname( plugin_basename(__FILE__) );
}
// function to call after plugin activation
function install()
{

}
}
```

Initializing the plugin is performed by creating a new instance of our class. This creates a $SnazzyArchives object:

```
// create new instance of the class
$SnazzyArchives = new SnazzyArchives();
```

We also want to execute a function when our plugin is activated, so we will use the register_activation_hook() API function. We need to specify the callback function using a reference to our newly created object. This is because the install() function is a member of our class.

```
// create new instance of the class
$SnazzyArchives = new SnazzyArchives();

if (isset($SnazzyArchives))
{
    // register the activation function by passing the reference to
    your instance
    register_activation_hook( __FILE__, array(&$SnazzyArchives,
    'install') );
}
```

We have the basics covered, and we can now move on to show our archives. First, we will cover how to display output on WordPress pages.

> **Quick reference**
>
>
>
> class_exists(): Useful PHP function to check if the class exists before doing anything with it. For the functions we have the function_exists() PHP functions.
>
> register_activation_hook(file, callback): Registers a plugin function to be run when the plugin is activated.

Showing template output with shortcodes

There are basically three ways to show output on a page in WordPress.

We have already covered the first one, using a content filter to insert the content into a page. This is what we have used in Chapter 2 with Digg This plugin.

The second method involves using shortcodes. Shortcode API was first introduced in WordPress 2.5. It basically behaves like the content filter internally, but allows you more options with less effort. An example shortcode is `[gallery]`, inserted into the post editor.

The third method involves calling our output function directly from the theme template.

Let's cover shortcodes first, as they provide an easy and powerful way to display dynamic content.

Time for action – Use a shortcode

1. Add a `display()` function to our class:

```
function display()
{
    return "Hello World!";
}
```

2. Add the `shortcode` function handler:

```
function SnazzyArchives()
{
    $this->plugin_url = trailingslashit( WP_PLUGIN_URL.'/'.
    dirname( plugin_basename(__FILE__) ) );

    // add shortcode handler
    add_shortcode('snazzy-archive', array(&$this, 'display'));
}
```

3. That's all! Using shortcodes is very easy.

Type in the shortcode `[snazzy-archive]` on any page:

4. WordPress will replace the shortcode with the output of our shortcode function right away:

What just happened?

We used a shortcode to display an example output on a WordPress page. Shortcodes are simple tags that you enter in the post editor. The shortcode API then automatically replaces the shortcode with the output of the functions associated with the shortcode.

To register a shortcode, you need to use the `add_shortcode()` function:

```
add_shortcode('snazzy-archive', array(&$this, 'display'));
```

The first parameter is a shortcode identifier (this is what you will use in post within brackets) and the second one specifies the handler function. In our case, it is the `display()` function in our class.

The handler function is always responsible for returning the content, which will replace the shortcode in post.

Shortcode API

We have just seen how shortcode API provides a powerful mechanism for displaying content in posts and pages. Although it works internally, very much like the content filter, it provides useful built-in functionalities that make it easier to use.

For example, a shortcode can accept parameters like this:

```
[gallery id="55" size="small" mode="1"]
```

The parameters are sent to the shortcode handling function as an associative array.

```
function display( $params )
{
    // $params is array( 'id' => '55', 'size' => 'small',
    'mode'=>'1')
}
```

Although you could parse the parameters manually, shortcode API also provides a function to do this, including setting default values. The function is `shortcode_atts( $defaults_array, $params )`.

It parses the incoming parameters and assigns default values to any missing parameter. It will also filter out all unwanted parameters.

Let 's see an example:

```
function display( $params )
{
    $values = shortcode_atts( array
    (
```

```
        'id' => '1',
        'size' => 'medium',
        'effect'=> '1'
    ), $params );
}
```

If we use the `[gallery id="55" size="small" mode="1"]` shortcode, the `$values` variable would contain `array ( 'id' => '55', 'size' => 'small', 'effect'=>'1')` after parsing and the `mode` parameter will be disregarded, as it is not provided in the default array.

Enclosing shortcodes

Shortcodes can also enclose content, and are written in the following format:

```
[gallery] content [/gallery]
```

The function `content` is treated as a part of shortcode, and will be replaced, along with the entire shortcode, with the output of the handling function. The enclosed content is passed as a second argument:

```
function display( $params, $content = null )
{
    if (!is_null($content))
        return $content ;
    else
        return 'Hello World !';
}
```

You can of course mix the shortcode parameters with the enclosed content:

```
[gallery id="55" ] content [/gallery]
```

Quick reference

`add_shortcode( string, handler )`: Assigns a handler function for the shortcode identified by a string

`shortcode_atts( defaults_array, params )`: Parses the shortcode parameters using a default array

More up to date information on the Shortcode API is available at: `http://codex.wordpress.org/Shortcode_API`.

Custom templates

The main advantage of shortcodes is their ease of implementation and use.

But sometimes, in order to achieve a desired output, we need more control over the output page. In the case of shortcodes and content filters, we are bound by the theme template.

We can overcome this limitation by creating a custom template page.

Time for action – Create a custom template

1. Create a `snazzy-template.php` file.

```php
<?php
/*
Template Name: Snazzy Archives
*/
?>

<?php get_header(); ?>

<div id="content">
    <p align="center">
        <?php if (isset($SnazzyArchives)) echo
        $SnazzyArchives->display(); ?>
    </p>
</div>

<?php get_footer(); ?>
```

2. Upload this file to your current theme folder.

3. When you create a page, you are now enable to select our template for the page:

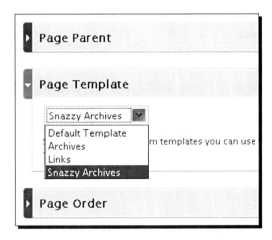

4. The page will now show how to use our template (without sidebar, page title):

What just happened?

We have just created a custom template for our theme. It allows us full control of the output page.

In order to declare a new template, you need to specify only the template name, and it will appear in the menu.

```php
<?php
/*
Template Name: Snazzy Archives
*/
?>
```

The rest of the template is normal HTML code. Normally, you would include the header and the footer of the theme, and WordPress provides the `get_header()` and `get_footer()` functions to display them.

Usually, using shortcodes will get the job done, but it is always useful to know other possibilities when we need broader control of the layout.

Quick function reference

`get_header()`, `get_footer()`, `get_sidebar()`: These are WordPress **include tags** and can be used within a template file to include other portions of the theme template such as header and footer.

You can also include any file from the current theme folder using:

```php
<?php include (TEMPLATEPATH . '/custom.php'); ?>
```

More information on template include files: `http://codex.wordpress.org/Include_Tags`

Prepare archives

Now that we have the page set up, we can begin with modifying our display() function to show all the posts.

The function will get the posts from the database, sorted by date (newest to oldest), and then print them using a predefined layout.

We want to name all our archive elements appropriately in the layout, so we can use CSS and jQuery later.

Every column will represent one whole month of post archives. Each month will have different days when postings occurred, and each day may have several posts for that day. Each post will have a title, image (if available) and excerpt text.

Below is a diagram of the archive structure with CSS div elements used.

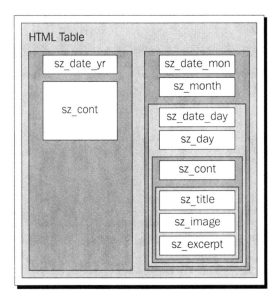

The structure we have in mind looks something like this:

Time for action – Show archives of posts

Let's modify our `display()` function to retrieve all the posts from the database.

1. Modify the existing `display()` function to print the general elements of the page:

```
function display()
{
    global $wpdb;

    // these variables store the current year, month and date
    processed
    $curyear='';
    $curmonth='';
    $curday='';
```

```
// the beginning of our output
    $result='
      <div class="snazzy">
        <table cellspacing="15" cellpadding="0" border="0">
          <tbody>
            <tr>'
```

2. Next, extract all the posts from the database using the `$wpdb` variable we covered in the previous chapter:

```
// query to get all published posts
$query="SELECT * FROM $wpdb->posts WHERE post_status =
'publish' AND post_password='' ORDER BY post_date_gmt DESC ";
$posts = $wpdb->get_results($query);
```

3. Then for each post we will retrieve title, excerpt, URL, and date:

```
foreach ($posts as $post)
{
    // retrieve post information we need
    $title = $post->post_title;
    $excerpt= $this->get_excerpt($post-
    >post_content);
    $url=get_permalink($post->ID);
    $date = strtotime($post->post_date);

    // format the date
    $day = date('d', $date);
    $month = date('M', $date);
    $year = date('Y', $date);
```

4. We will use a regular expression to search for an image in the post and store the URL in the `$imageurl` variable:

```
// look for image in the post content
$imageurl="";
preg_match('/<\s*img [^\>]*src\s*=\s*[\""\'']?([^\""\'\'>]*)
/i' , $post->post_content, $matches);
$imageurl=$matches[1];
```

5. We are also interested in getting the number of comments for the particular post:

```
// get comments for this post
$comcount = $wpdb->get_var("
    SELECT COUNT(*)
    FROM $wpdb->comments
    WHERE comment_approved = '1'
```

```
        AND comment_post_ID=$post->ID
        AND NOT (comment_type = 'pingback'
        OR comment_type = 'trackback')
        ");
");
```

6. Next comes the HTML formatting to create all our HTML elements:

```
// additional formatiing
if ($year!=$curyear)
{
    // close the previous day/month
    if ($curday)
    $result.="</div></div></td>";

    $curday='';
    $curmonth='';

    // year start in a new column (<td>)
    $result.= '<td valign="top"><div class="sz_date_yr">'
    .$year.'</div><div class="sz_cont">';

    $result.= '</div></td>';
    $curyear=$year;
}

if ($month!=$curmonth)
{
    // close the previous day/month
    if ($curday)
      $result.="</div></div></td>";

      $curday='';
    // month starts in a new column (<td>)
    $result.= '<td valign="top"><div class="sz_date_mon">'
    .$month.'</div><div class="sz_month">';

    $curmonth=$month;
}

if ($day!=$curday)
{
    // close previous day
    if ($curday)
      $result.="</div>";

    $result.= '<div class="sz_date_day">'.$day.'
    </div><div class="sz_day">';
    $curday=$day;
}
```

7. To print out the details of the post, we will use an external template:

```
// retrieve the archive entry representation
ob_start();
include('snazzy-layout-1.php');
$output = ob_get_contents();
ob_end_clean();

$result.=$output;
}
```

8. And finally, we close the page elements and return the result:

```
// close the previous day/month
if ($curday)
$result.="</div></div></td>";

// close the main page elements
$result.="</tr></tbody></table></div>";

// return the result
return $result;
}
```

9. We referenced a function to get the post excerpt, so we need to write it too:

```
function get_excerpt($text, $length = 15)
{
    if (!$length)
        return $text;

    $text = strip_tags($text);
    $words = explode(' ', $text, $length + 1);
    if (count($words) > $length)
    {
        array_pop($words);
        array_push($words, '...');
        $text = implode(' ', $words);
    }
    return $text;
}
```

10. And finally, let's create a layout file, `snazzy-layout-1.php`. Our template will output necessary classes (for example page or post), include the image if it exists, and output the content:

```
<div  class="sz_cont sz_img <?php echo ( ( $post->post_type=='page' )
? "sz_page" : "sz_post" ) ?>" <?php echo $imageurl ?
'style="background: transparent url('.$imageurl.') no-repeat
```

```
center;"' : '' ?>  >
    <a href="<?php echo $url ?>" title="<?php echo ($comcount ?
    "$comcount comments" : "") ?>" class="<?php echo $imageurl ?
    "sz_titleon" : "sz_title" ?>"><?php echo $title ?></a>
        <?php if ($excerpt && !$imageurl) : ?>
            <div class="sz_excerpt">&#8220;<?php echo $excerpt
            ?>&#8221;</div>
        <?php endif;?>
</div>
```

11. The end result of this somewhat lengthy code is the archives page that starts to look like our desired output.

| 2008 | Jul
20
Snazzy Archives
"Create a unique visual
representation of your blog's
archives!"
10
Snazzy Archive | Jun
30
WP Wall
"Add a Wall to your blog! WP Wall is
Ajax powered widget for your
sidebar, allowing ..."
15
Live Blogroll
"This plugin will liven up your
Blogroll by adding dynamic preview
of the posts from ..."
03
Digg this plugin
"Digg this plugin adds a nice Digg
button to all blog posts. Users can
submit ..."
01
About
"This is an example of a WordPress
page, you could edit this to put
information ..." | May
30
Hello world!
"Welcome to WordPress. This is
your first post. Edit or delete it,
then start blogging!" |

What just happened?

The `display()` function is now capable of extracting and showing all posts using our layout.

The whole archive view is encapsulated into a div and a table:

```
// the beginning of our output
$result='
  <div class="snazzy">
    <table cellspacing="15" cellpadding="0" border="0">
    <tbody>
    <tr>';

// MAIN ARCHIVE CONTENT

  // close the main page elements
    $result.="</tr></tbody></table></div>";
```

Get all posts from database

We can get a list of all previous posts with a WordPress database query. We want published posts, without a password, and sorted by date:

```
// query to get all published posts
    $query="SELECT * FROM $wpdb->posts WHERE post_status =
    'publish' AND post_password='' ORDER BY post_date_gmt DESC ";
    $posts = $wpdb->get_results($query);
```

We then retrieve the relevant post information. Notice that whenever we call a function in our class, we use `$this` reference, for example, `$this->get_excerpt()`:

```
// retrieve post information we need
    $title = $post->post_title;
    $excerpt= $this->get_excerpt($post->post_content);
    $url=get_permalink($post->ID);
    $date = strtotime($post->post_date);
```

Using a regular expression

In order to find an image in the post content, we use a regular expression, (`regexp`).

 Regular expressions are very powerful tools for searching patterns in content, although you do not need to know everything about them. The snippets of code like the ones we used are available throughout the Internet, and you just need to search for them (for example, you can find `regexp` for searching links on a page or checking if the email address is valid).

This `regexp` basically searches for the `<img />` tag in the content and returns the URL of the image, which we will use to display the picture:

```
// look for image in the post content
  $imageurl="";
  preg_match('/<\s*img [^\>]*src\s*=\s*[\""\']?([^\""\'>]*)/i',
  $post->post_content, $matches);
  $imageurl=$matches[1];
```

Retrieve comment count for a post

Here we have a snippet of code to get the comment count for a certain post. We are making sure that the comments are approved, and we do not want to count trackbacks or pingbacks.

```
// get comments for this post
  $comcount = $wpdb->get_var("
    SELECT COUNT(*)
```

```
        FROM $wpdb->comments
        WHERE comment_approved = '1'
        AND comment_post_ID=$post->ID
        AND NOT (comment_type = 'pingback'
        OR comment_type = 'trackback')
    ");
```

`$wpdb->get_var` is useful when we are retrieving only one variable from the database, in this case, `COUNT()` of the comments.

Using output buffers

The external file, `snazzy-layout-1.php`, contains the HTML representation of our archive entry.

In this case, we need to catch the output of the file and add it to our `$result` variable, because we are returning it at the end of the function.

That is why we use the output buffering PHP `ob_` functions:

```
// retrieve the archive entry representation
  ob_start();
  include('snazzy-layout-1.php');
  $output = ob_get_contents();
  ob_end_clean();
```

The `ob_start()` function will turn on output buffering, and while it is active, no content from the script will be sent to the output. Instead, it is stored in the internal buffer. The contents of this internal buffer may be retrieved by calling the `ob_get_contents()` function, and when we don't need it anymore, we can call the `ob_end_clean()` function to discard the buffer.

Apply styling and jQuery to archives

When we have all the data we need structured in HTML elements, it is quite easy to create the desired look with CSS. Here is an example:

Time for action – Style the archive view

Let's create a styling sheet for our archive.

1. Create a `snazzy-archives.css` file.

```
.snazzy
{
  text-align:left;
```

```
    overflow:auto;
  }

.snazzy_img
{
  margin:0;
  padding:0;
}

.sz_cont
{
  width:100px;
  display:block;
  overflow:hidden;
  margin:0px 0px 10px;
}

.sz_page
{
  bacground-color: #ffffef;
}

.sz_img
{
  height:110px;
}

.sz_year
{
  font-size:22px;
  color:#444;
  font-family:georgia, verdana;
  font-style:italic;
}

.sz_date_yr
{
  height:42px;
  font-size:34px;
}

.sz_date_mon
{
  height:29px;
  font-size:22px;
  cursor:pointer;
}

.sz_date_day
{
  background: #efefea;
```

```css
  margin-bottom:1px;
  height:20px;
  font-size:14px;
  font-weight:bold;
  cursor:pointer;
}

.sz_title
{
  padding:5px 0px;
  font-weight:bold;
  color:#444;
}

.sz_titleon
{
  line-height:14px;
  color:#eee;
  background-color:#333;
}

.sz_excerpt
{
  font-size:9px;
  padding-bottom:5px;
  color:#999;
}
```

2. Add an action for the `wp_print_scripts` event inside the class constructor to load our style sheet:

```php
// Initialize the plugin
function SnazzyArchives()
{
    $this->plugin_url=trailingslashit( get_bloginfo('wpurl')
    ).PLUGINDIR.'/'. dirname( plugin_basename(__FILE__) );

    // add shortcode handler
    add_shortcode('snazzy', array(&$this, 'display'));

    // print scripts action
    add_action('wp_print_scripts',  array(&$this,
    'scripts_action'));
}
```

3. The action will print out the reference to our style sheet:

```
function scripts_action()
{
    echo '<link rel="stylesheet" href="'.$this->plugin_url =
    trailingslashit( WP_PLUGIN_URL.'/'.
    dirname( plugin_basename(__FILE__) );
}
```

4. Once everything is prepared, we are ready to upload the files and take a look at a new archive page, freshly styled with CSS:

What just happened?

We used CSS to style our archive elements, such as the year, month and day headers, and the entire post layout.

We control the width of the entire column with only the width property of the post container, sz_cont, so it is easy to change.

```
.sz_cont
{
  width:100px;
  display:block;
  overflow:hidden;
  margin:0px 0px 10px;
}
```

Styling leaves endless possibilities for the user to play with. Let's also add interactivity using jQuery.

Time for action – Use jQuery to allow user interaction

As always, jQuery allows us to add powerful effects to our plugin with ease.

In this case, we want the ability to fold up months and days when we click on the date header. This way, we can hide the information we do not wish to read, for example, entire months.

1. Create the snazzy-archives.js file.

```
jQuery(document).ready(function($)
{
  $('.sz_date_mon').click(function()
  {
      $(this).next('.sz_month').children('.sz_day').toggle();
  });
  $('.sz_date_day').click(function()
  {
      $(this).next('.sz_day').slideToggle();
  });
});
```

2. Add our script to the scripts_action() function

```
function scripts_action()
{
    wp_enqueue_script('jquery');
    wp_enqueue_script('snazzy', $this->plugin_url.'/
```

```
snazzy-archives.js', array('jquery'));
echo '<link rel="stylesheet" href="'.$this->plugin_url.
'/snazzy-archives.css" type="text/css" />';
}
```

3. And that's all. We can now fold up the segments of the archive by simply clicking on months and days, and our jQuery code takes care of the rest:

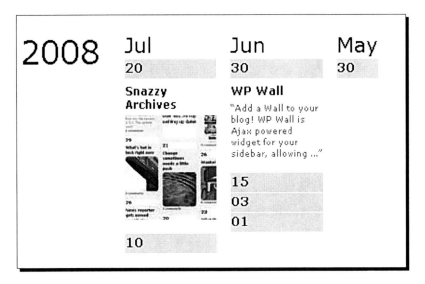

What just happened?

We used the power of jQuery to add interactivity to our archive page, using only a few lines of code.

The first snippet uses jQuery next and children selectors to toggle all the days (children of month div) inone of the following months, when the user clicks the month header:

```
$('.sz_date_mon').click(function()
{
    $(this).next('.sz_month').children('.sz_day').toggle();
});
```

The next snippet slides the day up and down when a certain day is clicked, using the jQuery slideToggle effect:

```
$('.sz_date_day').click(function()
{
    $(this).next('.sz_day').slideToggle();
});
```

These simple additions greatly increase the usability of the plugin with little effort from our side. But the requirement was structuring the plugin output properly and planning ahead.

Have a go Hero

When you have all the page elements you can now try to:

◆ Style the entire archive view to have fixed width and height (you could add width and height to `snazzy div`).

◆ Create a different layout file for displaying the post information in different ways. For example, you could make all the days the same height and write text above the pictures:

◆ Change the template to include buttons that would toggle the display all posts or pages when clicked (hint: using `$('.sz_post').toggle()` will do).

Creating plugin options page

It is always useful if the plugin allows you to customize it to your liking. Using external CSS and layout files makes it easier, but what about variables and functions we use in the code?

That is where the plugin options page comes to play. It can be loaded with settings that we can change, and is easily accessible from the WordPress administration panel.

Let's create a few options for our plugin:

- Allow the user to choose whether they want to display posts, pages, or both
- Start the archive view in mini mode
- Allow the user to provide descriptions for each year

The options page may look like this:

Snazzy Archives

Usage

Create a new page for your snazzy archive, and insert the code **[snazzy-archive]** into the post. Additionaly you may use the page template provided with the plugin.

Options

You can choose what pages you want to show in the archives.

☑ Show Posts
☐ Show Pages

Display

Mini mode can gain you a lot of space, and the user can expand/shrink archives by clicking on the date headings.

☐ Start in mini mode (collapsed archives)

Year book

You can specify unique text to print with any year, describing it. Year book shows below the year and is useful for sharing your thoughts.

Use description in the form year#description, one per line, HTML allowed.

```
2008#So far so good!



```

Update

In order to have an options page, we need to cover several key functionalities:

- Manage our options
- Set up the options page
- Show the options
- Save them after user input

It is actually easier than it may appear to be, and there is no excuse not to have an options page in our plugins anymore!

Time for action – Create an options page

1. First, we will declare the names for our options in the WordPress database:

```
class SnazzyArchives
{
    // this variable will hold url to the plugin
    var $plugin_url;

    // name for our options in the DB
    var $db_option = 'SnazzyArchives_Options';
```

2. We want to have a function for retrieving the plugin options. This function will also be able to set default values:

```
// handle plugin options
function get_options()
{
    // default values
    $options = array
    (
        'years' => '2008#So far so good!',
        'mini' => '',
        'posts' => 'on',
        'pages' => ''
    );
    // get saved options
    $saved = get_option($this->db_option);
    // assign them
    if (!empty($saved))
    {
        foreach ($saved as $key => $option)
        $options[$key] = $option;
    }
```

```
    // update the options if necessary
    if ($saved != $options)
      update_option($this->db_option, $options);

    //return the options
    return $options;
  }
```

3. We will set the default options when the plugin is activated. Use the `install()` function that we created earlier:

```
// Set up everything
function install()
{
    // set default options
    $this->get_options();
}
```

4. Next, let's create a function for handling our options page. It will parse and save the options when the user submits them, and is also responsible for showing the options using a layout saved in an external file:

```
// handle the options page
function handle_options()
{
    $options = $this->get_options();

    if ( isset($_POST['submitted']) )
    {

      //check security
      check_admin_referer('snazzy-nonce');

      $options = array();

      $options['years']=htmlspecialchars($_POST['years']);
      $options['layout']=(int) $_POST['layout'];
      $options['mini']= $_POST['mini'];
      $options['posts']= $_POST['posts'];
      $options['pages']= $_POST['pages'];

      update_option($this->db_option, $options);

      echo '<div class="updated fade"><p>
      Plugin settings saved.</p></div>';
    }

    $layout=$options['layout'];
    $years=stripslashes($options['years']);
    $mini=$options['mini']=='on'?'checked':'';
```

```
        $posts=$options['posts']=='on'?'checked':'';
        $pages=$options['pages']=='on'?'checked':'';
        // URL for form submit, equals our current page
        $action_url = $_SERVER['REQUEST_URI'];
        include('snazzy-archives-options.php');
}
```

5. We will edit the options page in an external file, `snazzy-archives-options.php`:

```html
<div class="wrap" style="max-width:950px !important;">
  <h2>Snazzy Archives</h2>

  <div id="poststuff" style="margin-top:10px;">

    <div id="mainblock" style="width:710px">

      <div class="dbx-content">
        <form action="<?php echo $action_url ?>" method="post">
          <input type="hidden" name="submitted" value="1" />
            <?php wp_nonce_field('snazzy-nonce'); ?>

          <h3>Usage</h3>
          <p>Create a new page for your snazzy archive, and
          insert the code <strong>[snazzy-archive]</strong>
          into the post. Additionaly you may use the page
          template provided with the plugin. </p>
          <br />

          <h3>Options</h3>
          <p>You can choose what pages you want to show in the
          archives.</p>
          <input type="checkbox" name="posts"  <?php echo $posts
          ?> /><label for="posts"> Show Posts</label>  <br />
          <input type="checkbox" name="pages"  <?php echo $pages
          ?> /><label for="pages"> Show Pages</label>  <br />
          <br />

          <h3>Display</h3>
          <p>Mini mode can gain you a lot of space, and the user
          can expand/shrink archives by clicking on the date
          headings.</p>
          <input type="checkbox" name="mini"  <?php echo
                                                 $mini ?>
          /><label for="mini"> Start in mini mode (collapsed
          archives)</label>  <br />
          <br />

          <h3>Year book</h3>
```

```
            <p>You can specify unique text to print with any
            year, describing it. Year book shows below the year
            and is useful for sharing your thoughts.</p>
            <p>Use description in the form year#description, one
            per line, HTML allowed. </p>
            <textarea name="years"  rows="10" cols="80"><?php echo
            $years ?></textarea>
            <br />

            <div class="submit"><input type="submit" name="Submit"
            value="Update" /></div>
        </form>
    </div>

  </div>

 </div>

</div>
```

This is basically an HTML form that submits data back to the script.

6. In order for our options page to show in the menu, we need to tell WordPress
which function it should call when the menu is displayed. We will do that using the
`add_options_page` function in the `admin_menu` filter:

```php
// Initialize the plugin
function SnazzyArchives()
{

    $this->plugin_url = trailingslashit( WP_PLUGIN_URL.'/'.
    dirname( plugin_basename(__FILE__) );

    // content filter
    add_filter('the_content',  array(&$this, 'content_filter'));

    // add shortcode handler
    add_shortcode('snazzy-archive', array(&$this, 'display'));

    // add options Page
    add_action('admin_menu',  array(&$this, 'admin_menu'));

}

// hook the options page
function admin_menu()
{

    add_options_page('Snazzy Archives Options', 'Snazzy Archives',
        8, basename(__FILE__), array(&$this, 'handle_options'));

}
```

This makes our options page operational, and can now be seen in the administration menu:

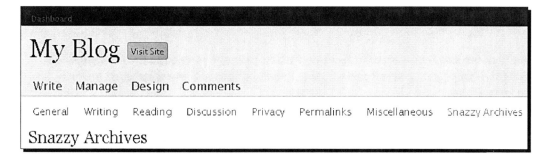

What just happened?

We have used WordPress API functions to create and install our options page in the administration panel.

In order to do that, we hooked into the `admin_menu` event and supplied our function:

```
add_action('admin_menu', array(&$this, 'admin_menu'));
```

This function registers our options page using the `add_options_page()` WordPress API call. This will create a menu item in the Administration panel using the name and file we pass to it.

```
// hook the options page
function admin_menu()
{
    add_options_page('Snazzy Archives Options', 'Snazzy Archives', 8,
    basename(__FILE__), array(&$this, 'handle_options'));
}
```

Managing plugin options

To manage plugin options, we are using a dedicated function, `get_options()`. Its purpose is to store default options, provide easy upgradeability (with new options in the future versions of the plugin) and return the current options.

It contains the default set of options we want to use:

```
function get_options()
{
    // default values
    $options = array
    (
        'years' => '2008#So far so good!',
```

```
        'mini' => '',
        'posts' => 'on',
        'pages' => ''
);
```

We then retrieve the saved options from the database and merge them with the default options. If there are no saved options, the default options will be copied over, and will become active.

```
// get saved options
$saved = get_option($this->db_option);
    // assign them
    if (!empty($saved))
    {
        foreach ($saved as $key => $option)
        $options[$key] = $option;
    }
```

Finally, we save the merged options and return them:

```
    // update the options if necessary
    if ($saved != $options)
    {
        update_option($this->db_option, $options);

        //return the options
        return $options;
    }
```

To install the default options, we make sure that the get_options() is called when the plugin is activated, and that is what our install() function was created for:

```
    // Set up everything
    function install()
    {
        // set default options
        $this->get_options();
    }
```

Handling options form

When you visit the options page, our external template is loaded and shown:

```
    function handle_options()
    {
        include('snazzy-archives-options.php');
    }
```

To fill the values in the template, we retrieve the options from the database and assign them to the local variables that are used in the template.

```
function handle_options()
{
  $options = $this->get_options();

  $layout=$options['layout'];
  $years=stripslashes($options['years']);
  $mini=$options['mini']=='on'?'checked':'';
  $posts=$options['posts']=='on'?'checked':'';
  $pages=$options['pages']=='on'?'checked':'';

  include('snazzy-archives-options.php');
}
```

To handle submits, we need to provide a path to the script. We can use the PHP `$_SERVER['REQUEST_URI']` variable:

```
$posts=$options['posts']=='on'?'checked':'';
$pages=$options['pages']=='on'?'checked':'';

// URL for form submit, equals our current page
  $action_url = $_SERVER['REQUEST_URI'];

  include('snazzy-archives-options.php');
}
```

When the user submits the form, we check the nonce and then save all the fields:

```
function handle_options()
{
    $options = $this->get_options();

      if ( isset($_POST['submitted']) )
      {
        //check security
        check_admin_referer('snazzy-nonce');

        $options = array();

        $options['years']=htmlspecialchars($_POST['years']);
        $options['mini']= $_POST['mini'];
        $options['posts']= $_POST['posts'];
        $options['pages']= $_POST['pages'];

        update_option($this->db_option, $options);

        echo '<div class="updated fade"><p>Plugin settings
        saved.</p></div>';
      }

      $layout=$options['layout'];
```

The way our page works is by directly connecting variables on the form with variables in the options.

For example, the `$posts` variable keeps the value of the option to show posts. The `POST` method would pass the value on for the checkbox if it was selected, and that is what we have saved in the database:

```
$options['posts']= $_POST['posts'];
```

When the template is shown, we assign the value `checked` to it if it had been selected previously:

```
$posts=$options['posts']=='on'?'checked':'';
```

In the template, we then print the value of the variable. If it had been checked earlier, the checkbox will be selected:

```
<input type="checkbox" name="posts" <?php echo $posts ?> /><label
for="posts"> Show Posts</label> <br />
```

Adding administration pages

WordPress administration menus are structured in a hierarchy of main menu pages and menu subpages.

Some examples of main menu pages are **Manage**, **Settings**, **Plugins**, **Write**, and **Users**. Submenu pages appear below these pages, for example, our plugin options page in the **Plugins** menu.

The function for adding main menu pages is:

```
add_menu_page(page_title, menu_title, access_level/capability,
 file, [function])
```

- ◆ `page_title`: Text that will go into the HTML of the page, as the title for the page when the menu is active
- ◆ `menu_title`: The on-screen name text for the menu
- ◆ `access_level/capability`: The minimum user level or the capability required to display and use this menu page
- ◆ `file`: The PHP file that handles the display of the menu page content
- ◆ `function`: The function that displays the page content for the menu page

If we want to add submenus, the format is similar:

```
add_submenu_page(parent, page_title, menu_title,
access_level/capability, file, [function]);
```

The only difference is in the `parent` parameter. It is the filename of the core WordPress admin file that supplies the top-level menu in which you want to insert your submenu (if this submenu is going into a custom top-level menu for example, `index.php`, `post.php`, `edit.php`, `themes.php`, `plugins.php`, and so on) or your plugin file.

For the most used main menus, WordPress provides functions for easier management of submenus:

- `add_management_page`: For adding submenus in the **Manage** menu

  ```
  // Add a new submenu under Manage:
  add_management_page('Test Manage', 'Test Manage', 8,
  'testmanage', 'manage_page');
  ```

- `add_options_page`: For adding submenus in the **Settings** menu

  ```
  // Add a new submenu under Options:
  add_options_page('Test Options', 'Test Options', 8,
  'testoptions', 'options_page');
  ```

- `add_theme_page`: For adding submenus in the **Design** menu

- `add_users_page`: For adding submenus in the **Users** menu

A few more examples are:

```
// Add a new top-level menu
add_menu_page('Test Toplevel', 'Test Toplevel', 8, __FILE__,
'toplevel_page');
// Add a submenu to the custom top-level menu:
add_submenu_page(__FILE__, 'Test Sublevel', 'Test Sublevel', 8,
'sub-page', 'sublevel_page');
```

Quick reference

`add_options_page(page_title, menu_title, access_level/capability, file)`: Adds a page in the **Settings** menu of the WordPress admin panel.

For the most up-to-date information on adding administration menus visit `http://codex.wordpress.org/Adding_Administration_Menus`.

Use plugin options

Now, we have created and stored the following options for our plugin:

- Select whether to show posts and/or pages
- Start the archive in collapsed mode
- Set the year descriptions

We should now modify the plugin to make a good use of them.

Time for action – Apply the plugin options

To select whether we want to show post or pages, we will modify the `display()` function.

1. Let's start by selecting whether to show posts and pages:

```
// the beginning of our output
$result='
    <div class="snazzy">
        <table cellspacing="15" cellpadding="0" border="0">
            <tbody>
                <tr>';

$options=$this->get_options();

//parse post options
$types=array();
if ($options['posts'])
    array_push($types, "'post'");
if ($options['pages'])
    array_push($types, "'page'");

$types=implode(',', $types);

// query to get all published posts
$query="SELECT * FROM $wpdb->posts WHERE post_status =
'publish' AND post_password='' AND post_type IN ($types)
ORDER BY post_date_gmt DESC ";

$posts = $wpdb->get_results($query);
```

2. To get the year's description we need to parse what the user entered in the text area:

```
$options=$this->get_options();
// parse year descriptions
if (!empty($options['years']))
{
  $yrs = array();
  foreach (explode("\n", $options['years']) as $line)
  {
    list($year, $desc) = array_map('trim', explode("#",
    $line, 2));
    if (!empty($year)) $yrs[$year] = stripslashes($desc);
  }
}

//parse post options
$types=array();
```

3. And then we display the year text below the year date in the table:

```
$result.= '<td valign="top"><div class=
"sz_date_yr">'.$year.'</div><div class="sz_cont">';

if ($yrs[$year])
  $result.='<div class="sz_year">&#8220;'.
  $yrs[$year].'&#8221;</div>';

$result.= '</div></td>';
```

4. Finally, when we want to start the view in mini mode, we need to pass this parameter to our jQuery script, which will handle this functionality.

```
function scripts_action()
{
    $options = $this->get_options();

    $mini=$options['mini'] ? 1 : 0;

    wp_enqueue_script('jquery');
    wp_enqueue_script('snazzy', $this->plugin_url . '/
    snazzy-archives.js', array('jquery'));

    // JavaScript options
    wp_localize_script('snazzy', 'SnazzySettings',
    array('snazzy_mini' => $mini));
```

5. Edit the `snazzy-archives.js file` and add the code to hide all the days if the `snazzy_mini` variable is set:

```
jQuery(document).ready(function($)
{
  snazzy_mini=parseInt(SnazzySettings.snazzy_mini);

  if (snazzy_mini)
  $('.sz_day').hide();

  $('.sz_date_mon').click(function()
  {
    $(this).next('.sz_month').children('.sz_day').toggle();
  });
```

We are done! Let's try it now. Turn all the options on, as shown:

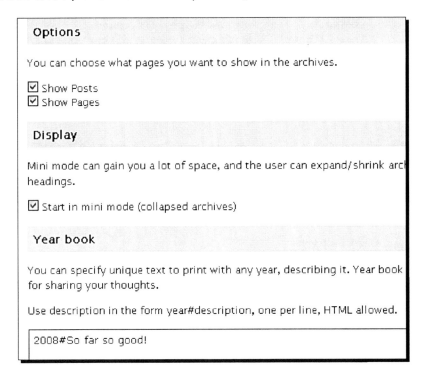

This will result in a collapsed archive view, showing both posts and pages and the year description we filled in:

What just happened?

We have included the functionality for the options we stored earlier.

We modify our query for posts based on whether we selected to show posts, pages or both, by using array manipulation routines:

```
$types=array();
if ($options['posts'])
  array_push($types, "'post'");
```

```
if ($options['pages'])
  array_push($types, "'page'");
$types=implode(',', $types);
```

We also display the description for each year, by parsing the input string. The following code splits the input string (`explode("\n", $options['years']`) and then applies the `trim()` to the year and the description using `array_map()`.

```
if (!empty($options['years']))
{
  $yrs = array();
  foreach (explode("\n", $options['years']) as $line)
  {
    list($year, $desc) = array_map('trim', explode("#",
    $line, 2));
    if (!empty($year)) $yrs[$year] = stripslashes($desc);
  }
}
```

The end result is an array `$yrs`, where keys are years and values are descriptions for that year. We can then use it to show the description for the years:

```
if ($yrs[$year])
  $result.='<div class="sz_year">&#8220;'.
  $yrs[$year].'&#8221;</div>';
```

Caching the plugin output

Let's learn how we can implement simple caching for our plugins. Caching is done in order to lessen the strain on the server and provide faster loading time for the user. This is especially true for blogs with large archives.

Time for action – Create archives cache

1. Add the variable to store the cache file path. We will use WordPress `wp-content` folder:

    ```
    // name for our options in the DB
      var $db_option = 'SnazzyArchives_Options';

    // path to store the cache file
      var $cache_path;

    // Initialize the plugin
      function SnazzyArchives()
      {
    ```

```
$this->plugin_url = trailingslashit( WP_PLUGIN_URL.'/'.
dirname( plugin_basename(__FILE__) ) );
$this->cache_path = ABSPATH .'wp-content/';
```

2. Next, we want to check if the cached content is present at the beginning of our `display()` function. If it is present, we will simply show that file to the user, skipping the dynamic creation of archives:

```
function display()
{
    global $wpdb;

    // try to retrieve cache
    $data = @file_get_contents($this-
    >cache_path."snazzy_cache.htm");

    // return the cache data if it exists
    if ($data)
      return $data;

    // these variables store the current year, month and
    date processed
    $curyear = '';
```

3. If the cache is not present, we will generate the archives as normal. Only this time, we want to save the cache file once it it's created.

```
    // close the main page elements
    $result .= "</tr></tbody></table></div>";

    // write cache
    if (is_writeable($this->cache_path))
    @file_put_contents($this->cache_path."snazzy_cache.htm",
    $result);

    // return the result
    return $result;
```

4. That will serve as the basic cache functionality. In order to delete the cache every time a change has been made (post has been added or edited), we will add the following code to our class constructor to initialize the `delete_cache` function:

```
    // add options Page
    add_action('admin_menu', array(&$this, 'admin_menu'));
    // delete output cache
    add_action( 'edit_post',  array(&$this,'delete_cache'));
    add_action( 'save_post',  array(&$this,'delete_cache'));
}
```

5. Finally, we need to code the function. It will simply delete the file from the server:

```
function delete_cache()
{
    @unlink($this->cache_path."snazzy_cache.htm");
}
```

What just happened?

We created a simple caching mechanism that is able to retrieve the cached file from the server, create it if it does not exist, and remove the cache after a post has been changed or added.

The cached file is retrieved from the disk using the `file_get_contents` command (@ sign before the function name will suppress all the warning messages, for example, a message that the file does not exist):

`$data = @file_get_contents($this->cache_path."snazzy_cache.htm");`

The file is written in the same way as if the content has been dynamically generated. Here, we introduce another WordPress function `is_writeable`, which can check if the given path is writeable by the server:

```
if (is_writeable($this->cache_path))
  @file_put_contents($this->cache_path."snazzy_cache.htm", $result);
```

We also used two new actions `edit_post` and `save_post`, which are executed when the post is edited or saved:

```
// delete output cache
  add_action( 'edit_post',  array(&$this,'delete_cache'));
  add_action( 'save_post',  array(&$this,'delete_cache'));
```

Have a go Hero

Once you have the options panel installed, you may add more enhancements to the plugin.

You can try a few:

- Option to turn caching ON/OFF
- Option to select different layouts (which you will create!) for presenting the archive
- Allow the user to select the time period for showing archives
- Exclude the specific posts from the archives by their IDs

Summary

With the Snazzy archives plugin, we created a unique way for users to show their archives. The plugin output can be customized using CSS, layout files, and the options page.

We have learned how to manipulate the layout of the template using shortcodes and custom templates. This allows us to show the output the way we want it.

It is a great usability bonus for the plugin when it has an options page. And another important lesson we learned was how to manage options, and how to create option pages easily.

Let's sum up what we learned in this chapter:

- **Classes**: We can learned how to use classes, properties and methods to write our plugins.
- **Shortcodes**: The shortcode API provides a powerful mechanism for changing content.
- **Custom templates**: These allow us to fully control the layout of the page.
- **Manage Options**: We learned how to manage our plugin options, including setting default values.
- **Administrative menus**: We added an administration page, and learned how to insert our pages into WordPress menus.
- **File caching**: This provides a method to cache the plugin output.

We will continue to create exciting plugins in the next chapter as well. Our next one will automatically find relevant Flickr images and YouTube videos for your post, and allow you to insert them into a post with a single click!

6
Insights for WordPress

The previous chapters explored WordPress features visible on the site including modifying and sending output to the pages and the sidebar. In this chapter, we are going to deal more with the modification of the administration panel.

How many times, while writing a post, have you needed to refer one of your previous articles? It is a time consuming job—searching the article on your blog to get a link. The plugin we are about to create will make finding your old posts take only a couple of seconds.

Everyone knows that a picture is worth a thousand words. So we will also learn how to find and insert relevant Flickr photos into your articles as well.

This chapter is all about digging a little deeper into the WordPress and hacking the **Write Post** screen.

You will learn to create custom panels in the various sections of the Write Post screen. Also, you will learn how to access the current WordPress rich editor, tinyMCE, and create a button on its toolbar. You will also learn how to interact with Flickr API that allows you access to the world's largest images repository.

Let's sum up what awaits us:

- ◆ **Creating custom panels** in the Write Post screen
- ◆ **Searching your posts** based on keywords
- ◆ Accessing **Flickr** and search for relevant photos
- ◆ Inserting content into the **WordPress editor** directly
- ◆ Adding a **tinyMCE plugin and a button**

And you will do all of these by creating the **Insights** plugin to access your articles and Flickr images quickly from within the WordPress edit page.

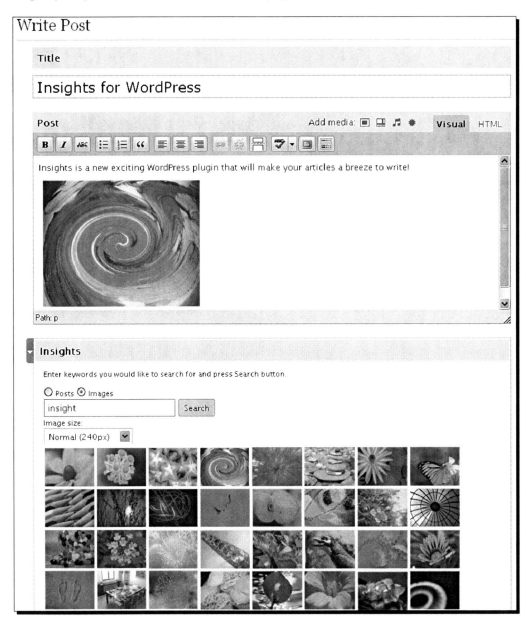

We have a lot to do, so let's get going!

Creating custom panels in the editor screen

The first part of our plugin will cover integration of images into the WordPress **Write Post** screen.

We want to add a custom panel, which we will use later to display the search results.

Time for action – Create a new plugin outline

Let's start building our plugin by creating a PHP class, and then adding functionality to create a custom panel.

1. Create a new folder called insights.

2. Create a new file, `insights.php`.

```php
<?php
/*
Plugin Name: Insights
Version: 0.1
Plugin URI:
        http://www.prelovac.com/vladimir/wordpress-plugins/insights
Author: Vladimir Prelovac
Author URI: http://www.prelovac.com/vladimir
Description: Quickly find relevant posts and Flickr images for
             your article
*/
global $wp_version;
$exit_msg='Insights for WordPress requires WordPress 2.6 or
     newer. <a href="http://codex.wordpress.org/Upgrading_
     WordPress">Please update!</a>';
if (version_compare($wp_version,"2.6","<"))
{
    exit ($exit_msg);
}
// Avoid name collisions.
if ( !class_exists('WPInsights') ) :
class WPInsights
{
    // name for our options in the DB
    var $DB_option = 'WPInsights_options';
    // the plugin URL
    var $plugin_url;
    // Initialize WordPress hooks
    function WPInsights()
    {
```

```
            $this->plugin_url = trailingslashit( WP_PLUGIN_URL.'/'.
            dirname( plugin_basename(__FILE__) );
        }
        // Set up everything
        function install()
        {
        }
}
endif;
if ( class_exists('WPInsights') ) :
    $WPInsights = new WPInsights();
    if (isset($WPInsights))
    {
        register_activation_hook( __FILE__,
        array(&$WPInsights, 'install') );
    }
endif;
?>
```

We have set up up a framework for our new plugin.

3. Let's add the custom panel to the **Write Post** screen. First, we need to hook into the admin menu:

```
function WPInsights()
{
    $this->plugin_url = trailingslashit( WP_PLUGIN_URL.'/'.
    dirname( plugin_basename(__FILE__) );
    // admin_menu hook
    add_action('admin_menu',  array(&$this, 'admin_menu'));
}
```

4. Now, add our custom panels using the WordPress add_meta_box function and specifying our function responsible for drawing the panel:

```
// Hook the admin menu
function admin_menu()
{
    // custom panel for edit post
    add_meta_box( 'WPInsights', 'Insights', array
    (&$this,'draw_panel'), 'post', 'normal', 'high' );
    // custom panel for edit page
    add_meta_box( 'WPInsights', 'Insights', array
    (&$this,'draw_panel'), 'page', 'normal', 'high' );
}
```

5. For now, our `draw_panel` will just write a simple text:

```
// draw the panel
function draw_panel()
{
    echo 'Hello World!';
}
```

That's all! You can see our new panel in the **Write Post** (and **Page**) screens. It's in the box just below the editor window.

The panel automatically has all the styles of the other core WordPress panels. Also, it inherits JavaScript, so you can open and close it just like all the other panels. And like most good things we did it in just a few lines of code!

What just happened?

Just as in the previous chapter, we are using a class to outline our plugin with default properties such as a name for the plugin option and a variable to hold the plugin URL.

```
class WPInsights
{
// name for our options in the DB
    var $DB_option = 'WPInsights_options';
    // the plugin URL
    var $plugin_url;
}
```

To access and add content to WordPress panels, we use the available API function `add_meta_box()`:

```
function admin_menu()
{
    // custom panel for edit post
    add_meta_box( 'WPInsights', 'Insights', array
    (&$this,'draw_panel'), 'post', 'normal', 'high' );
    // custom panel for edit page
    add_meta_box( 'WPInsights', 'Insights', array
    (&$this,'draw_panel'), 'page', 'normal', 'high' );
}
```

The function takes the identifier and the title of the panel. Also, you can specify a callback function to draw the panel—in our case, we named it `draw_panel()`.

```
function draw_panel()
{
  echo 'Hello World!';
}
```

For now, we just output a simple text, but we will soon add more functionality to it.

Custom edit panels in WordPress

Typically, WordPress allows us to insert a panel in one of the three sections of the editor screens outlined below:

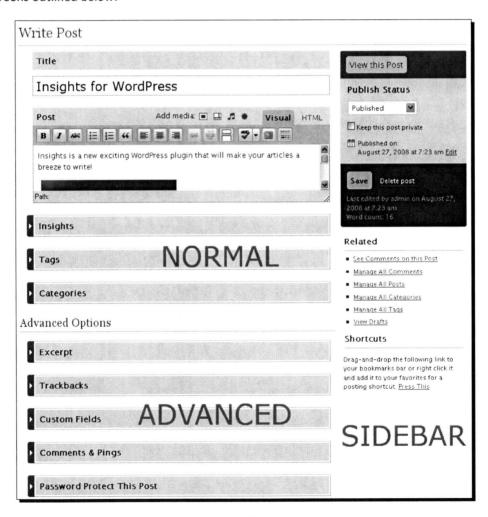

The first one is called **Normal**, and is just below the post editor. It contains the most frequently used panels such as post Categories and Tags.

The second section is called **Advanced**, and is located below the normal section with core panels such as Excerpts and Custom Fields.

The third section is the **Sidebar**, where we can add panels below the WordPress sidebar content.

Using jQuery, we can insert panels almost anywhere. But currently only those three sections are covered with the API. The WordPress API also allows us to choose the order in which the panels are shown, by assigning them priority.

Let's take a close look at the `add_meta_box()` function:

```
add_meta_box(id, title, callback, page, section, priority)
```

- `id`: It allows us to refer to the panel in the document later.
- `title`: It is the title of the box.
- `callback`: It is a function that fills the box with the desired content. The function should echo its output.
- `page`: It is the type of edit page on which to show the box (post, page, link)
- `section`: It is the section within the page where the boxes should show (for example 'normal' or 'advanced')
- `priority`: It is the priority within the section where the boxes should be shown ('high', 'core', 'default', 'low')

For example, let's create our panel in the advanced section of the post screen, using default priority:

```
add_meta_box( 'WPInsights', 'Insights', array(&$this,'draw_panel'),
'post', 'advanced', 'default' );
```

The `add_meta_box()` function does not support adding panels to the sidebar yet, but you can use the `submitpost_box` action instead:

```
add_action('submitpost_box', array( &$this, 'my_sidebar' ) );
function my_sidebar()
{
  echo '<p> Hello World! </p>';
}
```

Related

- See Comments on this Post
- Manage All Comments
- Manage All Posts
- Manage All Categories
- Manage All Tags
- View Drafts

Shortcuts

Drag-and-drop the following link to your bookmarks bar or right click it and add it to your favorites for a posting shortcut. Press This

Hello World!

In the upcoming versions of WordPress, we are likely to see a unified function for all the sections, so keep an eye on WordPress Codex.

Quick function reference

`add_meta_box(id, title, callback, page, section,`
`priority)`: Add panels to the sections of editor pages (post, page and link). Codex link: `http://codex.wordpress.org/Function_Reference/`
`add_meta_box`

`submitpost_box`: Action to add panel to the sidebar

Searching the posts

Our next functionality will involve displaying a list of all posts that match a given keyword, which will involve searching our database.

Time for action – Display a list of matching posts

> *1.* Modify our `draw_panel()` function to show an input field:
>
> ```
> // draw the panel
> function draw_panel()
> {
> ```

```
echo '
<p>Enter keywords you would like to search for and press the
Search button.</p>

<input type="text" id="insights-search" name="insights-
search" size="25" autocomplete="off" />
<input id="insights-submit" class="button" type="button"
value="Search"  />';
}
```

This gives us an input box and a **Search** button to work with.

2. We will also add a div to display the search results in:

```
<input id="insights-submit" class="button" type="button"
value="Search"  />';

echo '<div id="insights-results"></div>';
}
```

3. Let's add input handling functionality and Ajax. Create a file, `insights.js`.

   First, let's add a function to submit the query using Ajax.

```
// Insights for WordPress plugin

// setup everything when document is ready
jQuery(document).ready(function($)
{
    // initialize the variables
    var last_query=undefined;

    // function to submit rhe query and get results
    function submit_me()
    {
        // check if the search string is empty
        if ($('#insights-search').val().length==0)
        {
            $('#insights-results').html('');
```

```
                        return;
                }
                // create the query
            var query = InsightsSettings.insights_url + '/insights-
        ajax.php?search=' + escape($('#insights-search').val())+
        '&mode=' + mode + '&_ajax_nonce=' +
                    InsightsSettings.nonce;;
            // check if already called
            if (query!=last_query)
            {
                $('#insights-results').html('Please wait...');
                $('#insights-results').load(query);
                last_query=query;
            }
        }
    });
```

4. Now, let's add responses to the *ENTER* key and **Search** button click:

```
// search button click event
$('#insights-submit').click(function()
{
    submit_me();
});
// check for ENTER or ArrowDown keys
$('#insights-search').keypress(function(e)
{
    if (e.keyCode == 13 || e.keyCode == 40)
    {
        submit_me();
        return false;
    }
});
});
```

5. We need to declare our script as always. This time, we are using a functionality that enables us to decide on which admin pages we want the script to be shown on. Edit the constructor of our class:

```
function WPInsights()
{
    $this->plugin_url = trailingslashit( WP_PLUGIN_URL.'/'.
    dirname( plugin_basename(__FILE__) );

    // admin_menu hook
```

```
add_action('admin_menu', array(&$this, 'admin_menu'));

// print scripts action
add_action('admin_print_scripts-post.php', array(&$this,
'scripts_action'));
add_action('admin_print_scripts-page.php', array(&$this,
'scripts_action'));
add_action('admin_print_scripts-post-new.php', array(&$this,
'scripts_action'));
add_action('admin_print_scripts-page-new.php', array(&$this,
'scripts_action'));
}
```

6. Now, add the function to print our script and the URL parameter we use:

```
// prints the scripts
function scripts_action()
{
    $nonce=wp_create_nonce('insights-nonce');

    wp_enqueue_script('jquery');
    wp_enqueue_script('insights', $this->plugin_url.
    '/insights.js', array('jquery'));
    wp_localize_script('insights', 'InsightsSettings',
    array('insights_url' => $this->plugin_url, 'nonce' =>
    $nonce));

}
```

7. Finally, we need to create the Ajax response. Create a new file, `insights-ajax.php`, which will handle all Ajax search queries:

```
<?php
require_once('../../../wp-config.php');

if ($_GET['search'])
{
    // check security
    check_ajax_referer('insights-nonce');

    die(search_posts($_GET['search']));
}
else
    die('No results found.');

// search posts
function search_posts($search)
{
    global $wpdb, $WPInsights;
```

```php
        // create query
        $search = $wpdb->escape($search);
        $posts = $wpdb->get_results("SELECT ID, post_title,
        post_content FROM $wpdb->posts WHERE post_status = 'publish'
        AND (post_title LIKE '%$search%' OR post_content LIKE
        '%$search%') ORDER BY post_title LIMIT 0,5");

        //
        if ($posts)
        foreach ($posts as $post)
        {
            // display every post link and excerpt
            $output .= '
            <p>
                <a href="' . get_permalink($post->ID) . '"
                style="cursor:pointer;" >
                <strong>' . $post->post_title . '</strong>
                </a><br />
                ' . get_excerpt($post->post_content, 25) . '</p>';
        }
        else
            $output .= 'No posts matched "' .
            stripslashes($search) . '"';

            return $output;
    }

// get the content excerpt
function get_excerpt($text, $length = 25)
{
    if (!$length)
        return $text;

    $text = strip_tags($text);
    $words = explode(' ', $text, $length + 1);
    if (count($words) > $length)
    {
        array_pop($words);
        array_push($words, '...');
        $text = implode(' ', $words);
    }
    return $text;
}
?>
```

Putting all of this together, we will have created a functional Ajax search for the editor page, which can find posts for us in an instant!

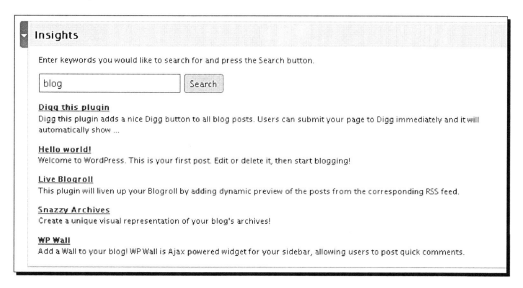

What just happened?

We will add our script to the WordPress admin pages using a method that allows us to decide which admin pages to print scripts on. To do that, you need to append the admin page name to the action name, as shown here:

```
add_action('admin_print_scripts-post.php',  array(&$this,
'scripts_action'));
add_action('admin_print_scripts-page.php',
array(&$this, 'scripts_action'));
add_action('admin_print_scripts-post-new.php',
array(&$this, 'scripts_action'));
add_action('admin_print_scripts-page-new.php',
array(&$this, 'scripts_action'));
```

The page names are `page.php` or `post-new.php` or any other WordPress admin page which you can see in your browser. Using this method, we avoid cluttering other pages with unnecessary scripts.

As always, we use jQuery to handle JavaScript events. In this case, we want to respond to the user clicking the search button and pressing the *Enter* or *Down Arrow* keys.

```
// search button click event
$('#insights-submit').click(function()
{
    submit_me();
```

```
});
// check for ENTER or ArrowDown keys
$('#insights-search').keypress(function(e)
{
    if (e.keyCode == 13 || e.keyCode == 40)
    {
        submit_me();
        return false;
    }
});
```

As you may notice, the `keypress` event returns `false` if the desired key was pressed, signaling to the browser that we've handled the event, and it should not be processed anymore.

If that was not the case, the *Enter* key would have submitted the entire post for saving, because our panel is placed within a WordPress edit post form (almost the whole page is).

That is also the reason why we used this method instead of creating our form (we did not want to create a nested form).

Our `submit_me()` function is a typical interface to an Ajax call. We added some simple optimization by testing if the search string was empty:

```
if ($('#insights-search').val().length==0)
{
```

And if the current query is different from the previously saved one:

```
if (query!=last_query)
```

The results are gathered by using the jQuery `load` method to call our external script:

```
$('#insights-results').load(query);
```

Our Ajax responder, `insights-ajax.php`, contains a function to search all the posts for a given keyword and return a list of post titles, links and excerpts.

Our keyword is first escaped and then run through a MySQL query using the `LIKE` directive to compare to post titles and content:

```
$search = $wpdb->escape($search);
$posts = $wpdb->get_results("SELECT ID, post_title, post_content
FROM $wpdb->posts WHERE post_status = 'publish' AND (post_title
LIKE '%$search%' OR post_content LIKE '%$search%') ORDER BY
post_title LIMIT 0,5");
```

We now have a list of links that we can copy and paste to the WordPress editor.

It is certainly much faster than before, but we can speed the things up by inserting the links directly into the WordPress tinyMCE editor.

Quick reference

`admin_print_scripts-post.php`: By referencing the page in the action name, the action will be called only on the given page, reducing the server load in the rest of the admin panel.

Interacting with tinyMCE

tinyMCE is a popular web-based WYSIWYG editor which WordPress uses for rich-text post editing. tinyMCE has a JavaScript interface which we will use to access common functions such as inserting the text directly to the editor.

Time for action – Insert the link into tinyMCE

1. Edit the `insights.js` file and add the functionality to insert the HTML directly into tinyMCE:

```
// Insights for WordPress plugin

// send html to the editor
function send_wp_editor(html)
{
    var win = window.dialogArguments || opener || parent || top;
    win.send_to_editor(html);

    // alternatively direct tinyMCE command for insert
    // tinyMCE.execCommand("mceInsertContent", false, html);
}
function insert_link(html_link)
{
    if ((typeof tinyMCE != "undefined") && ( edt = tinyMCE.
    getInstanceById('content') ) && !edt.isHidden() )
    {
        var sel = edt.selection.getSel();

        if (sel)
        {
            var link = '<a href="' + html_link + '" >' + sel
            + '</a>';

            send_wp_editor(link);
        }
    }
```

```
}
// setup everything when document is ready
jQuery(document).ready(function($)
{
```

2. Assign the `onclick` event to the output link in `insights-ajax.php`:

```
<p>
<a onclick="insert_link(\'' . get_permalink($post->ID) . '\');
 return false;"  style="cursor:pointer;"  >
<strong>' . $post->post_title . '</strong>
```

What just happened?

Because we included the `tinyMCE` integration, all you have to do now—to create a link—is to select some text on your blog, search for a matching post, and just click on it. The link will be automatically created. Something that took few minutes before now only takes a few seconds.

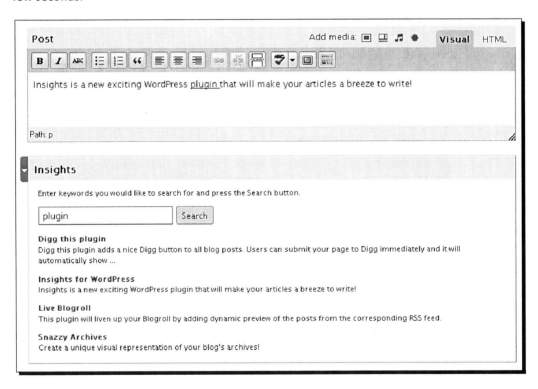

The post link is assigned the `onclick` event that sends the link to the `insert_link()` JavaScript function:

```
<a onclick="insert_link('http://scriptcopy.com/devblog/?p=114');
return false;"> Digg this plugin</a>
```

This function first checks if the tinyMCE editor is present:

```
function insert_link(html_link)
{
    if ((typeof tinyMCE != "undefined") && ( edt = tinyMCE.
    getInstanceById('content') ) && !edt.isHidden() )
    {
```

We then get the selected text, create an HTML link and send it to the `send_wp_editor()` function:

```
        if ((typeof tinyMCE != "undefined") && ( edt =
        tinyMCE.getInstanceById('content') ) && !edt.isHidden() )
        {
            var sel = edt.selection.getSel();
            if (sel)
            {
              var link = '<a href="' + html_link + '" >'
              + sel + '</a>';
              send_wp_editor(link);
            }
        }
    }
}
```

We used the WordPress built in `send_to_editor()` function (declared in `/wp-admin/js/media_upload.js`) to send HTML to the `tinyMCE` editor.

```
// send html to the editor
function send_wp_editor(html)
{
    var win = window.dialogArguments || opener || parent || top;
    win.send_to_editor(html);

    // alternatively direct tinyMCE command for insert
    // tinyMCE.execCommand("mceInsertContent", false, html);
}
```

Alternatively, we could have sent the data directly using tinyMCE's `mceInsertContent` command.

tinyMCE is a huge project on its own, and you can find more on `tinyMCE` commands and functions available at `http://tinymce.moxiecode.com/`.

Quick reference

TinyMCE: A standalone web-based HTML editor. Visit the TinyMCE documentation Wiki at: `http://wiki.moxiecode.com/index.php/TinyMCE:Index`.

Using Flickr API

Just as easily as we used the Digg API in our first plugin, we will use the Flickr API to enhance our Insights plugin further.

In order to use Flickr API, you need to first register for an API key at `http://www.flickr.com/services/api/keys/apply/`.

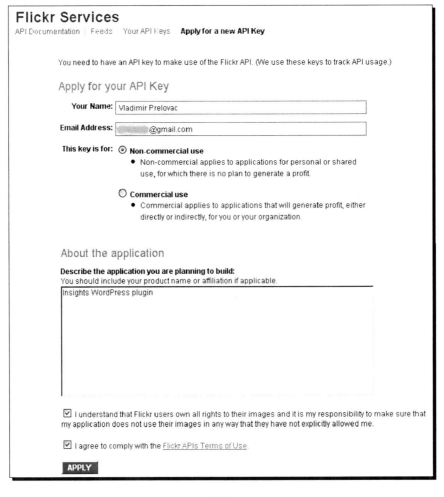

This in turn allows you to use all of the Flickr services including searching and uploading of photos.

In order to complete our plugin, we will need to learn how to use the search functionality of Flickr.

Time for action – Display Flickr photos

Let's introduce the Flickr API to our plugin. This will allow you to display a list of images from Flickr and insert them into your article with a click of a mouse!

1. Modify the `draw_panel()` function to include two radio checkboxes allowing us to select posts or images:

```
function draw_panel()
{
    echo '
    <p>Enter keywords you would like to search for and press the
    Search button.</p>

    <input name="insights-radio" type="radio" checked=""
    value="1" /><label> Posts </label>
    <input name="insights-radio" type="radio" value="2"/><label>
    Images </label>

    <br />

    <input type="text" id="insights-search" name="insights-
    search" size="25" autocomplete="off" />
```

2. The next step is to change the `submit_me()` function to include the preferred search mode in the query. So, we add another parameter named `mode`:

```
function submit_me()
{
    // check if the search string is empty
    if ($('#insights-search').val().length==0)
    {
        $('#insights-results').html('');
            return;
    }
    // get active radio checkbox
    var mode = $("input[@name='insights-radio']:checked").val();

    // create the query
    var query = InsightsSettings.insights_url + '/insights-
    ajax.php?search=' + escape($('#insights-search').val()) +
    '&mode=' + mode;

    // check if already called
    if (query!=last_query)
```

3. We also need to add a function to insert our image to the post, similar to how we handled links earlier:

```
// insert image to the editor
function insert_image(link, src, title) {

    var size = document.getElementById('img_size').value;
    var img = '<a href="' + link + '"><img src="' + src + size +
    '.jpg" alt="' + title + '" title="' + title + '" hspace="5"
    border="0" /></a>';

    send_wp_editor(img);
}
```

4. All that is left now is to make changes to our Ajax responder, `insights-ajax.php`, in order to include Flickr support.

Let's start with parsing the mode parameter. If the mode is 2, we select the image search:

```
if ($_GET['search'])
{

  // check security
    check_ajax_referer('insights-nonce');

    if ($_GET['mode'] == '2') // mode 2 is image search
      die(search_images($_GET['search']));
    else
      die(search_posts($_GET['search']));
}
else
  die('No results found.');
```

5. Next, let's create a function to handle Flickr photos. Since Flickr allows searching of images by both tag and description, we will include both the methods for better results:

```
// handle Flickr photos
  function search_images($keyword)
  {
      // search by tags
      $tag_images = search_flickr($keyword, 'tags' );
      // search by description
      $text_images = search_flickr($keyword, 'text');
```

6. Flickr allows us to see photos in several different predefined sizes, so we will add a selection box before the images, to select the size we want to use in our article:

```
// if any results
if ($tag_images || $text_images)
{
    // output image size selection box
    $output = '
    Image size:<br /><select id="img_size">
    <option value="_s">Thumbnail (75px)</option>
    <option value="_t">Small (100px)</option>
    <option value="_m" selected="selected">Normal (240px)</option>
    <option value="">Medium (500px)</option>
    <option value="_b">Large (1024px)</option>
    </select>
    <br />';

    // output images
    if ($tag_images)
      $output .= $tag_images;

    if ($text_images)
      $output .= $text_images;
}
else
    $output = 'No images matched "' . stripslashes($keyword) . '"';

    return $output;
}
```

7. Finally, we need the function to interact with Flickr—send the query, parse the response and create the output. All that is handled by one function:

```
// call the Flickr Api
  function search_flickr($keyword, $mode = 'tags', $count = 16)
  {
      // prepare Flickr query
      $params = array(
      'api_key' => '72c75157d9ef89547c5a7b85748106e4',
      'method' => 'flickr.photos.search',
      'format' => 'php_serial',
      'tag_mode' => 'any',
      'per_page' => $count,
      'license' => '4,6,7',
      'sort' => 'interestingness-desc',
      $mode => $keyword);
      $encoded_params = array();
```

```php
foreach ($params as $k => $v)
{
    // encode parameters
    $encoded_params[] = urlencode($k) . '=' . urlencode($v);
}

// call the Flickr API
$url = "http://api.flickr.com/services/rest/?" .
        implode('&', $encoded_params);

$rsp = wp_remote_fopen($url);

// decode the response
$rsp_obj = unserialize($rsp);

// if we have photos
if ($rsp_obj && $rsp_obj['photos']['total'] > 0)
{
  foreach ($rsp_obj['photos']['photo'] as $photo)
  {
    // link to photo page
    $link = 'http://www.flickr.com/photos/' .
    $photo['owner'] . '/' . $photo['id'];

      // img src link
      $src = 'http://farm' . $photo['farm'] .
      '.static.flickr.com/' . $photo['server'] . '/' .
      $photo['id'] . '_' . $photo['secret'];

      // create output
      $output .= '<img hspace="2" vspace="2" src="' . $src .
      '_s.jpg" title="' . $photo['title'] . '" onclick=
      "insert_image(\'' . $link . '\', \'' . $src . '\', \''
      . str_replace("'", "&acute;", $photo['title']) . '\');"
      />';
  }
}

    return $output;
}
```

And the final result is a collection of photos meeting our search criteria:

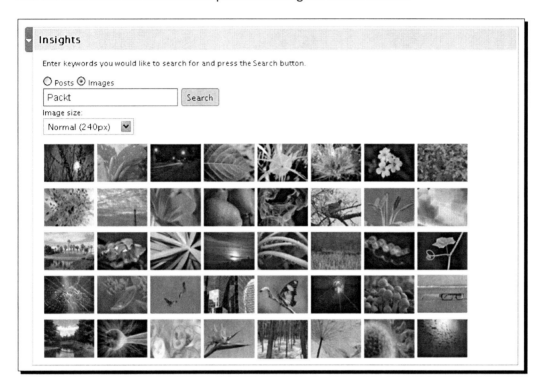

What just happened?

We used the Flickr API to get a collection of photos matching our search phrase.

Using the API is easy—thanks to the extensive Flickr API documentation and lots of examples. In our case, we used the `flickr.photos.search` method with additional parameters:

```
// call the Flickr Api
function search_flickr($keyword, $mode = 'tags', $count = 16)
{
    // prepare Flickr query
    $params = array(
    'api_key' => '72c75157d9ef89547c5a7b85748106e4',
    'method' => 'flickr.photos.search',
    'format' => 'php_serial',
    'tag_mode' => 'any',
    'per_page' => $count,
    'license' => '4,6,7',
    'sort' => 'interestingness-desc',
    $mode => $keyword);
```

We can select how many photos we want (per page), what the format of the response should be (format), how the images should be sorted (sort), and many other options.

Calling the API is a simple matter of using a URL:

```
// call the Flickr API
$url = "http://api.flickr.com/services/rest/?" . implode('&',
$encoded_params);

$rsp = wp_remote_fopen($url);
```

Since we asked for for `php_serial` data, we can use the `unserialize()` function to parse the Flickr response:

```
// decode the response
$rsp_obj = unserialize($rsp);
```

Finally, we create output based on the data we get from Flickr in a predefined form:

```
// if we have photos
if ($rsp_obj && $rsp_obj['photos']['total'] > 0)
{
    foreach ($rsp_obj['photos']['photo'] as $photo)
    {
      // link to photo page
      $link = 'http://www.flickr.com/photos/' . $photo['owner']
      . '/' . $photo['id'];

      // img src link
      $src = 'http://farm' . $photo['farm'] . '.static.
      flickr.com/' . $photo['server'] . '/' . $photo['id'] .
      '_' . $photo['secret'];
```

Since we assigned the `onclick` event to every photo, we can easily add them to our editor using the same tinyMCE functionality we used earlier.

```
      // create output
      $output .= '<img hspace="2" vspace="2" src="' . $src . '_s.
      jpg" title="' . $photo['title'] . '" onclick="insert_image
      (\'' . $link . '\', \'' . $src . '\', \'' . str_replace
      ("'", "&acute;", $photo['title']) . '\');" />';
    }
```

The user can select the size, and we retrieve the value of the selected box.

```
function insert_image(link, src, title)
{
    var size = document.getElementById('img_size').value;
```

To retrieve the picture with the given size, we only need to form the URL differently.

For every photo, we also create a link to the original author's page to attribute their work:

```
var img = '<a href="' + link + '"><img src="' + src + size +
'.jpg" alt="' + title + '" title="' + title + '" hspace="5"
border="0" /></a>';

send_wp_editor(img);
}
```

And now with a click of the mouse, we can add a photo to our post.

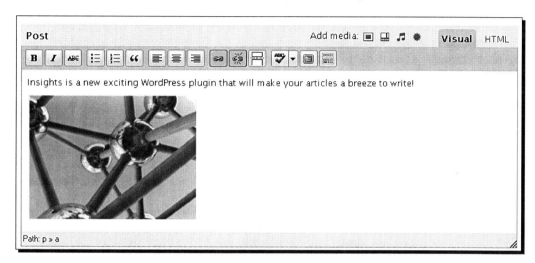

Quick reference

`Wp_remote_fopen($url)`: Get the contents of a remote page

Flickr API documentation: `http://www.flickr.com/services/api/`

Using third-party solutions—phpFlickr

Sometimes, there may be a possibility of using a third-party solution for your plugin; in this case, it was the excellent phpFlickr API. It contains a set of PHP functions that make it easy to handle Flickr functionalities.

Using an API like phpFlickr allows you to concentrate on top-level functions, while the API author will worry about any changes Flickr may have on their own API.

However, when using such a package, you also need to consider the following:

- You will still need to keep your plugin updated with the current version of the given package to preserve compatibility.

- The package will add to the size of your own plugin, in some cases considerably (the current phpFlickr package is almost 400 KB on its own!).

When making a decision on this, it is usually a compromise between speed and ease of development with the considerations mentioned above.

Creating a tinyMCE plugin

tinyMCE is such a big editor that supports plugins on its own.

We will create a **tinyMCE** button on the editor toolbar with assigned functionality.

In order to create a `tinyMCE` plugin, we need to follow the procedure as stated on the `tinyMCE` plugin documentation page (`http://wiki.moxiecode.com/index.php/TinyMCE:Create_plugin/3.x`) and also WordPress codex for implementing `tinyMCE` plugins within WordPress (`http://codex.wordpress.org/TinyMCE_Custom_Buttons`).

Time for action – Adding a button to tinyMCE

1. Let's start by adding WordPress related `tinyMCE handling`. **Edit our class constructor and add:**

```
add_action('admin_print_scripts-post-new.php', array(&$this,
'scripts_action'));
add_action('admin_print_scripts-page-new.php', array(&$this,
'scripts_action'));
// add tinyMCE handlig
add_action( 'init', array( &$this, 'add_tinymce' ) );
}
```

2. This function will add the necessary filters to handle the plugin and the button:

```
function add_tinymce()
{
    if ( ! current_user_can( 'edit_posts' ) && ! current_user_can
    ( 'edit_pages' ) )
    return;

    if ( get_user_option('rich_editing') == 'true' )
    {
        add_filter( 'mce_external_plugins', array( &$this,
        'add_tinymce_plugin' ) );
        add_filter( 'mce_buttons', array( &$this,
        'add_tinymce_button' ));
    }
}
```

3. WordPress filters, `mce_external_plugins` and `mce_buttons`, are used to register the plugin and the button:

```
function add_tinymce_plugin( $plugin_array )
{
    $plugin_array['insights'] = $this->plugin_url. '
    /insights-mceplugin.js';
    return $plugin_array;
}

function add_tinymce_button( $buttons )
{
    array_push( $buttons, "separator", 'btnInsights' );
    return $buttons;
}
```

4. You will need to have a 20x20 image for your button. You can call it `button.gif` and save it in the `i/` folder ('i' for images).

5. The plugin itself is a JavaScript module in which you define commands and buttons. Let's create a file, `insights-mceplugin.js`:

```
// Insights tinyMCE 3 plugin

(function()
{
    tinymce.create('tinymce.plugins.Insights',
    {
        init : function(ed, url)
        {
          // Register the command so that it can be invoked by
            using tinyMCE.activeEditor.execCommand('mceInsights');
          ed.addCommand('mceInsights', function()
          {
            ed.windowManager.open
            ({
                file : url + '/insights-popup.php',
                width : 650,
                height : 520,
                inline : 1
            },
            {
                plugin_url : url, // Plugin absolute URL
            });
          });
        });
        // Register a button
```

```
        ed.addButton('btnInsights',
        {
          title : 'Insights',
          cmd : 'mceInsights',
          image : url + '/i/button.gif'
        });
    },
    // Returns information about the plugin as a name/value array.
    getInfo : function()
    {
        return
        {
            longname : 'Insights for WordPress',
            author : 'Vladimir Prelovac',
            authorurl : 'http://www.prelovac.com/vladimir',
            infourl : 'http://www.prelovac.com/vladimir/
            wordpress-plugins/insights',
            version : "0.1"
        };
    }
});
// Register plugin
tinymce.PluginManager.add('insights', tinymce.plugins.Insights);
})();
```

6. We will have a pop-up window when the button is pressed, so we also need a corresponding PHP file. Create the `insights-popup.php` file with simple content just for now:

```
<html>
<body>
    Hello World!
</body>
</html>
```

The result is the I button on the tinyMCE toolbar, which opens a specified document in a new window within our document.

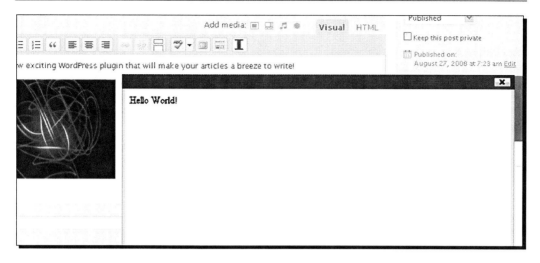

What just happened?

We have created a tinyMCE plugin which opens a window in our editor.

In order to hook our plugin and button into tinyMCE, we must first use the two WordPress tinyMCE filters, mce_external_plugins and mce_buttons:

```
add_filter( 'mce_external_plugins', array( &$this,
'add_tinymce_plugin' ) );
add_filter( 'mce_buttons', array( &$this, 'add_tinymce_button' ));
```

To declare the tinyMCE plugin, we need to provide the URL to the plugin.js file:

```
function add_tinymce_plugin( $plugin_array )
{
    $plugin_array['insights'] = $this->plugin_url. '/
    insights-mceplugin.js';
    return $plugin_array;
}
```

To add the button, we pass our button identifier to the function (the same as the one we used in the plugin.js file).

We also pass an extra separator button to separate our button from the rest:

```
function add_tinymce_button( $buttons )
{
    array_push( $buttons, "separator", 'btnInsights' );
    return $buttons;
}
```

The tinyMCE plugin JavaScript file is used to initialize the plugin and define its functionality.

We created a new `tinyMCE` command, and named it `mceInsights`. It opens a window with our `insights-popup.php`.

```
ed.addCommand('mceInsights', function()
{
    ed.windowManager.open
    ({
        file : url + '/insights-popup.php',
        width : 650,
        height : 520,
        inline : 1
    },
    {
        plugin_url : url, // Plugin absolute URL
    });
});
```

You can specify the width and the height of the new window. The `inline` parameter specifies if the file will be opened in the current document or in a new browser window.

The command function can be anything you want, and does not have to create a window at all. For example:

```
ed.addCommand('mceInsights',do_something);
```

Where `do_something` is a JavaScript function that is executed when the command is called.

To register a button, we need to declare a unique identifier, `btnInsights`, and associate the command, `mceInsights`, which will be executed when the button is clicked, on the path to the button image file, `/i/button.gif`.

```
// Register a button
    ed.addButton('btnInsights',
    {
        title : 'Insights',
        cmd : 'mceInsights',
        image : url + '/i/button.gif'
    });
```

That covers the creation of a **tinyMCE** button and a plugin. Let's move the functionality of our WordPress panel to the new window now.

Create a functional tinyMCE plugin window

Our tinyMCE window will be opened in a new frame or in a new window. This means that it will be a standalone HTML document.

So we will need to call all the necessary `.js` files such as jQuery and define all other elements of a HTML file.

Time for action – Open a tinyMCE window

Let's create an example tinyMCE window.

```php
<?php
require_once('../../../wp-config.php');
?>

<html xmlns="http://www.w3.org/1999/xhtml">
<head>
    <title>Insights</title>

    <script type='text/javascript'>
/* <![CDATA[ */
    var insights_url="<?php echo get_option('siteurl') ?>
    /wp-content/plugins/insights";
/* ]]> */
</script>

    <script type='text/javascript' src='<?php echo get_
option('siteurl') ?>/wp-includes/js/jquery/jquery.js'></script>

    <script type="text/javascript" src="<?php echo get_
option('siteurl') ?>/wp-content/plugins/insights/insights.js"></
script>

    <link rel="stylesheet" href="<?php echo get_option('siteurl')
?>/wp-includes/js/tinymce/themes/advanced/skins/wp_theme/dialog.
css?ver=311"/>

</head>

<body>
    <p>Enter keywords you would like to search for and press Search
button.</p>

    <input name="insights-radio" type="radio" checked="" value="1"
/><label> Posts </label>
    <input name="insights-radio" type="radio" value="2"/><label>
Images </label>
    <br />

    <input type="text" id="insights-search" name="insights-search"
size="25" />
```

```
    <input id="insights-submit" class="button" type="button"
value="Search" autocomplete="off" />

    <div id="insights-results"></div>
</body>
</html>
```

The result is a plugin form with a functionality similar to that of our original
WordPress panel. The two can exist together.

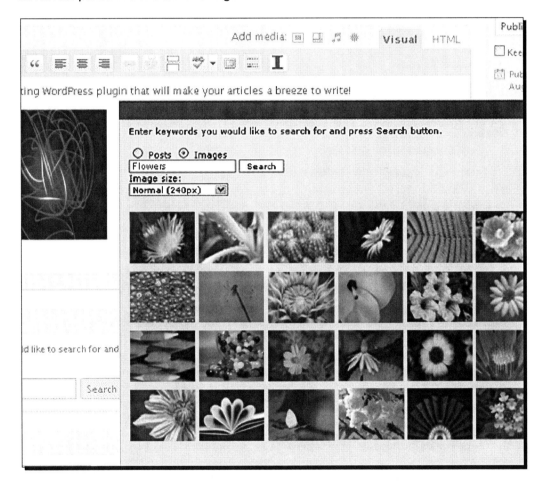

What just happened?

We created a new window within the editor, and because the window opens as a new
independent document, we need to specify all the required HTML elements.

That means we also need to manually include the necessary JavaScript files, jQuery and our `insights.js` file:

```
<script type='text/javascript' src='<?php echo get_option
('siteurl') ?>/wp-includes/js/jquery/jquery.js'></script>

<script type="text/javascript" src="<?php echo get_option
('siteurl') ?>/wp-content/plugins/insights/insights.js"></script>
```

We can see that this is not as elegant anymore as we are now stepping outside WordPress. So we lose a part of the functionality as well. Also, every time this window is opened, certain waiting time is involved as the scripts need to be read and parsed again. You may have already experienced that in working with the tinyMCE plugins.

On the other hand, you can transform the editor into virtually anything as it allows you to change almost every one of its aspects.

Quick reference

tinyMCE development links: `http://wiki.moxiecode.com/index.php/TinyMCE:Create_plugin/3.x`

`http://codex.wordpress.org/TinyMCE_Custom_Buttons`

`mce_external_plugins`, `mce_buttons`: WordPress filters for registering tinyMCE plugins and buttons

tinyMCE: A standalone web-based HTML editor. Visit the tinyMCE documentation Wiki at `http://wiki.moxiecode.com/index.php/TinyMCE:Index`

Have a go hero

Another plugin is behind us, and what a powerful one!

But with a plugin like this, it is also easy to find new features you could add.

For example:

◆ Creating the settings page with options to select the number of posts and images shown

◆ Enhancing the plugin with other search options such as YouTube videos, Wikipedia, Google Blog Search, and so on

Summary

Insights is a productivity enhancing plugin. We have seen how to improve the productivity of your post editor by hooking directly to the WordPress edit pages and using Ajax to generate fast searches.

Our plugin helps us find posts on our blog, so we can link to them quickly.

We discovered Flickr API and the ways to use it in order to show relevant images to decorate our posts with.

And finally, we learned how to integrate our plugin with the WordPress panels and the tinyMCE editor.

Let's underline the most important lessons from this chapter:

◆ **WordPress edit page**: Adding panels to the various sections of the WordPress edit page

◆ **tinyMCE integration**: Adding text to WordPress editor

◆ **tinyMCE buttons and plugins**: Creating a button directly on the tinyMCE editor toolbar and assigning it certain functionality

◆ **Search Flickr**: Flickr is the world's largest photo repository and we now know how to use it

WordPress has many uses but do you think can we turn it into a **CMS (Content Management System)**? Let's explore that with our final plugin.

7
Post Types

In our next (and final) plugin, we are going to dig even deeper into the WordPress engine and discover ways to further modify various aspects of the backend to match our specific needs.

We will also explore the possibility of turning WordPress into a **Content Management System** (**CMS**), using methods provided to us by WordPress.

Although WordPress is made primarily for the purpose of handling a blog, this basic functionality can be easily expanded to handle almost anything you want. The WordPress backend is very flexible, and can be customized to accommodate a lot of different purposes. For example, you could create a job portal or an e-commerce quite easily with WordPress, and those are just some of the possibilities.

In this chapter, you will learn how to:

- Implement **localization** support for users of other languages
- Customize **menus** and **submenus** to change the way the WordPress backend looks
- Handle **file** and **image** uploads
- Use **custom fields** to add custom hidden information to your posts
- Customize the **manage page** output
- Use the **error message** class to handle display of errors
- Use built-in **WordPress capabilities** to handle user permissions

And you will do all of these by developing a **Post Types** plugin that provide pre-defined post templates to add a photo or a link quickly to your blog.

The concepts you will learn in this chapter will help you discover the not so obvious capabilities of the WordPress platform that allows you to transform it into software—capable of handling much more than just a blog.

Handling localization

Localization is an important part of WordPress development as not everyone using WordPress speaks English (WordPress comes in different languages too).

Localization involves just a small amout of the extra work on your side, since the translation itself is usually done by volunteers (people who like and use your plugin).

You only need to provide some base files for translation, and don't be surprised when you start getting translated files sent to your inbox.

WordPress uses the **GNU gettext localization framework**, which is a standardized method of managing translations, and we will make use of it in our plugin.

Time for action – Create plugin and add localization

We will start by defining our plugin as usual, and then add localization support.

1. Create a new folder called `post-types`.

2. Create a new `post-types.php` file with the following content:

```php
<?php

// pluginname Post Types
// shortname PostTypes
// dashname post-types

/*
Plugin Name: Post Types
Version: 0.1
Plugin URI:
        http://www.prelovac.com/vladimir/wordpress-plugins/post-types
Author: Vladimir Prelovac
Author URI: http://www.prelovac.com/vladimir
Description: Provides pre-defined post templates to quickly add a
             photo or a link to your blog

*/

// Avoid name collisions.
if ( !class_exists('PostTypes') ) :

class PostTypes
{

    // localization domain
    var $plugin_domain='PostTypes';

    // Initialize the plugin
    function PostTypes()
    {
        global $wp_version;

        $exit_msg='Post Types requires WordPress 2.5 or newer.
        <a href="http://codex.wordpress.org/Upgrading_WordPress">
        Please update!</a>';
```

```
            if (version_compare($wp_version,"2.5","<"))
            {
                exit ($exit_msg);
            }

        }

        // Set up default values
        function install()
        {
        }
    }
endif;

if ( class_exists('PostTypes') ) :

    $PostTypes = new PostTypes();
    if (isset($PostTypes))
    {
        register_activation_hook( __FILE__, array(&$PostTypes,
        'install') );
    }
    endif;
```

3. Adding localization is fairly simple. First we need to add a function to our class that will load the translation file:

```
// Localization support
function handle_load_domain()
{
    // get current language
    $locale = get_locale();

    // locate translation file
    $mofile = WP_PLUGIN_DIR.'/'.plugin_basename(dirname
    (__FILE__)).'/lang/' . $this->plugin_domain . '-' .
    $locale . '.mo';

    // load translation
    load_textdomain($this->plugin_domain, $mofile);
}
```

4. Since loading the file takes resources, we will load it only when the translation is actually needed by checking the current page (`$pagenow`) and the list of pages pages where we need translations (`$local_pages` array):

```php
// Initialize the plugin
function PostTypes()
{
    global $wp_version, $pagenow;

    // pages where our plugin needs translation
    $local_pages=array('plugins.php');

    if (in_array($pagenow, $local_pages))
        $this->handle_load_domain();

    $exit_msg='Post Types requires WordPress 2.5 or newer.
    <a href="http://codex.wordpress.org/Upgrading_WordPress">
    Please update!</a>';
```

5. Finally, to use the available translations, we only need to enclose our text in the __() function:

```php
    $this->handle_load_domain();

    $exit_msg=__('Post Types requires WordPress 2.5 or newer.
    <a href="http://codex.wordpress.org/Upgrading_WordPress">
    Please update!</a>', $this->plugin_domain);

    if (version_compare($wp_version,"2.5","<"))
```

What just happened?

We have added localization support to our plugin by using the provided localization functions provided by WordPress.

Currently, we have only localized the error message for WordPress version checking:

```php
    $exit_msg=__('Post Types requires WordPress 2.5 or newer.
    <a href="http://codex.wordpress.org/Upgrading_WordPress">
    Please update!</a>', $this->plugin_domain);
```

We have done that by enclosing the text in the __() function, which takes the text as localized, and enclosing our unique localization domain or context within the WordPress localization files.

To load localization, we created a `handle_load_domain` function.

The way it works is to first get the current language in use by using the
get_locale() function:

```
// Localization support
function handle_load_domain()
{
    // get current language
    $locale = get_locale();
```

Then it creates the language file name by adding together the plugin dir, plugin folder, and the lang folder where we will keep the translations. The file name is derived from the locale, and the *.mo language file extension:

```
// locate translation file
$mofile = WP_PLUGIN_DIR.'/'.plugin_basename
(dirname(__FILE__)).'/lang/' . $this->plugin_domain .
'-' . $locale . '.mo';
```

Finally, the localization file is loaded using the load_textdomain() function, taking our text domain and .mo file as parameters.

```
// load translation
load_textdomain($this->plugin_domain, $mofile);
```

Optimizing localization usage

The translation file needs to be loaded as the first thing in the plugin—before you output any messages. So we have placed it as the first thing in the plugin constructor.

Since loading the translation file occurs at the beginning of the constructor, which is executed every time, it is a good idea to select only the pages where the translation will be needed in order to preserve resources.

WordPress provides the global variable, $pagenow, which holds the name of the current page in use.

We can check this variable to find out if we are on a page of interest. In the case of plugin activation error message, we want to check if we are on the plugins page defined as plugins.php in WordPress:

```
// pages where our plugin needs translation
$local_pages=array('plugins.php');

if (in_array($pagenow, $local_pages))
    $this->handle_load_domain();
```

You can optimize this further by querying the page parameter, if it exists, as this will—in most cases—point precisely to the usage of your page (`plugins.php?page=photo`):

```
if ($_GET['page']=='photo')
```

Optimizing the usage of the translation file is not required; it's just a matter of generally loading only what you need in order to speed up the whole system.

How does localization work?

For localization to work, you need to provide `.po` and `.mo` files with your plugins. These files are created by using external tools such as PoEdit, which we will cover in more detail in the next chapter.

These tools output the compiled translation file, which can be then loaded by using the `load_textdomain()` function. This function accepts a language domain name and a path to the file.

In order to use translated messages, you can use the `__($text, $domain)` and `_e($text, $domain)` functions. The `_e()` function is just an equivalent of

```
echo __();
```

These functions accept two parameters, the first being the desired text, and the second, the language domain where the message will be looked for.

If no translation was found, the text is just printed out as it is. This means that you can always safely use these functions, even if you do not provide any translation files. This will prepare the plugin for future translation.

Quick reference

`$pagenow`: A global variable holding the name of the currently displayed page within WordPress.

`get_locale()`: A function which gets the currently selected language.

`load_textdomain(domain, filepath)`: This function loads the localization file and adds it to the specified language domain identifier.

`__();` `_e()`: These functions are used to find the output text using a given language domain.

More information about WordPress localization is available at:
`http://codex.wordpress.org/Translating_WordPress`.

Adding a post template

Our next goal is to add a simple post template to the WordPress write page.

The purpose of a custom post template is to handle writing a quick post in case we don't need the whole Write Post interface, for reasons of speed or customization.

The great thing about post templates is that they can be customized to accept any information you want—for example, job portal listings or inventory items.

Let's start with a simple Add Photo template where we want to be able to just set the title, specify a photo and publish immediately.

Time for action – Create 'add photo' post template

1. In order to create the post template, we need a place for it in the menus. We will use the **Write** menu and place a submenu there:

```
// add admin_menu action
add_action('admin_menu', array(&$this, 'admin_menu'));
}
// Hook the admin menu
function admin_menu()
{
    // submenu pages
    add_submenu_page('post-new.php', __('Add Photo',
    $this->plugin_domain) , __('Photo', $this->plugin_domain) , 1 ,
    'add-photo', array(&$this, 'display_form') );
}
```

2. Since we have localized text on our new page, we want to make sure that the localization file is loaded on this page, so we will add it to our $local_pages array:

```
function PostTypes()
{
    global $wp_version, $pagenow;

    // pages where our plugin needs translation
    $local_pages=array('plugins.php', 'post-new.php');

    if (in_array($pagenow, $local_pages))
```

3. Let's create the template/ folder and call our new write post template, photo.php.

4. We will start the template with the boxes that display the information :

```
<div class="wrap">

  <?php    if (!empty($error)) : ?>
     <div id="message" class="error fade">
        <p><?php echo $error; ?></p>
     </div>
  <?php    elseif (!empty($published_id)) : ?>
    <div id="message" class="updated fade">
      <p><strong><?php _e('Photo added.',$this->plugin_domain);
      ?></strong> <a href="<?php echo get_permalink(
                                  $published_id);
      ?>"><?php _e('View post',$this->plugin_domain); ?>
      &raquo;</a></p>
    </div>
  <?php endif; ?>

  <h2><?php _e('Add Photo',$this->plugin_domain); ?></h2>
  <form action="" method="post" enctype="multipart/form-data">
  <?php wp_nonce_field($_GET['page']);
```

5. Then add the **Publish** button using the WordPress CSS classes:

```
<div id="poststuff">

<div class="submitbox" id="submitpost">
<div id="previewview"></div>
<div class="inside"></div>
  <p class="submit"><input name="publish" type="submit"
  class="button button-highlighted" tabindex="5" value="
  <?php _e('Publish', $this->plugin_domain); ?>" /></p>
</div>
```

6. Finally, we add the input fields to the template—title, photo URL or upload field, and description:

```
<div id="post-body">
<div id="titlediv">
  <h3><?php _e('Title',$this->plugin_domain); ?></h3>
<div id="titlewrap"><input type="text" name="title" tabindex
="1" value="<?php echo $title; ?>" id="title" /></div>
</div>
```

```
        <div class="postbox ">
          <h3><?php _e('Photo',$this->plugin_domain); ?></h3>
        <div class="inside">
          <p>
          <label for="url"><?php _e('Enter URL:
                    ',$this->plugin_domain);
          ?></label><br />
          <input style="width: 415px"  tabindex="2" type="text"
          name="url" id="url" value="<?php echo $url; ?>" />
          </p>
        <?php if ($uploadfile) : ?>
          <p>
          <label for="upload"><?php _e('or Upload Photo:',$this-
          >plugin_domain); ?></label><br />
          <input type="file"  tabindex="3" name="upload" id=
                                              "upload" />
          </p>
        <?php endif; ?>
        </div>
      </div>

      <div class="postbox">
        <h3><?php _e('Description (optional)'
                  ,$this->plugin_domain); ?>
        </h3>
      <div class="inside">
        <textarea name="description" id="description" rows="5"
         style="width: 415px" tabindex="4"><?php echo
         $description; ?>
        </textarea>
      </div>
      </div>


      </div>
      </div>
      </form>
    </div>
```

7. The template is done! To display it, we will create a `display_form()` function in our main plugin class.

```
// Display the Post form
function display_form()
{
    global $wpdb;
```

```
$page=$_GET['page'];
switch ($page) :
case 'add-photo':
include( 'template/photo.php');
break;
endswitch;
}
```

The function does not process any information yet; it just prints out the template.

The end result is our new post template in the **Write** menu.

What just happened?

We have just created a quick photo post template. For the sake of simplicity, the form has been designed to have only three fields.

When creating a backend form, you can design it any way you want, but you can also decide to use the WordPress CSS classes. If you go for WordPress classes, your forms will **blend** into the backend and look more professional.

Backend CSS classes

The standard classes of WordPress Backend CSS (up to version 2.6) use `wrap` for displaying forms, and use `poststuff` to create the wrapper.

`submitbox` is the righthand side column with the **Publish** button that contains extra classes such as `previewview` and `inside`, and the button itself is of the class, `submit`:

```
<div class="submitbox" id="submitpost">
<div id="previewview"></div>
<div class="inside"></div>
    <p class="submit"><input name="publish" type="submit"
      class="button button-highlighted" tabindex="5" value="
    <?php _e('Publish', $this->plugin_domain); ?>" /></p>
</div>
```

The main form classes are `post-body` followed by `titlediv` and `titlewrap` for handling post titles:

```
<div id="titlediv">
    <h3><?php _e('Title',$this->plugin_domain); ?></h3>
<div id="titlewrap"><input type="text" name="title" tabindex=
  "1" value="<?php echo $title; ?>" id="title" /></div>
</div>
```

Finally, we have `postbox` and `inside` for handling fields and groups of information:

```
<div class="postbox">
  <h3><?php _e('Description (optional)',$this->
  plugin_domain); ?></h3>
  <div class="inside">
    <textarea name="description" id="description" rows="5" style=
    "width: 415px" tabindex="4"><?php echo $description; ?>
    </textarea>
  </div>
</div>
```

Since the WordPress backend evolves quickly, you should check the styling classes on all the new versions and adjust your plugin accordingly.

Handling file and image uploads

WordPress provides ready functions for handling file uploads and image manipulation.

It is always best practice to use built-in WordPress functions for checking the file, moving it and setting file permissions. We will use these functions in the following example.

Time for action – Handle uploaded image

1. Let's add a function to handle images uploaded by the user. The function uses the built-in `wp_handle_upload()` function:

```
function handle_image_upload($upload)
{
    // check if image
    if (file_is_displayable_image( $upload['tmp_name'] ))
    {
        // handle the uploaded file
        $overrides = array('test_form' => false);
        $file=wp_handle_upload($upload, $overrides);
    }
    return $file;
}
```

2. Now, we need to include the image to our post. Let's expand the `display_form()` function to include handling of uploaded images and inserting a new post with attachment:

```
// Display the Post form
function display_form()
{
    global $wpdb;

    $page=$_GET['page'];
    $published=isset($_POST['publish']);
    $title=$_POST['title'];
    $description=$_POST['description'];

    if ($published)
    {
        check_admin_referer($page);
        $post_status='publish';
    }

    switch ($page) :

    case 'add-photo':
    // WordPress upload dir (wp-content/uploads)
```

```
$uploads = wp_upload_dir();
// check permissions
if (is_writable($uploads['path']))
{
  $uploadfile=true;
}
$url=$_POST['url'];
$upload=$_FILES['upload'];

if ($published)
{
  if (!empty($title) && (!empty($upload['tmp_name']) ||
  !empty($url)))
  {
    // if file uploaded
    if ($upload['tmp_name'])
      {
        // handle uploaded image
        $file=$this->handle_image_upload($upload);

        if ($file)
        {
          $image_url=$file['url'];

          // create a thumbnail
          $size='medium';
          $resized = image_make_intermediate_size( $file
          ['file'], get_option("{$size}_size_w"), get_option
          ("{$size}_size_h"), get_option("{$size}_crop") );

          if ($resized)
            $image_src=$uploads['url'] .'/'.$resized['file'];
          else
            $image_src=$image_url;

            $image_uploaded=true;
          }
          else
            $error=__('Please upload a valid image.',$this-
            >plugin_domain);
        }
        else // if file uploaded
        {
          $image_url=$url;
          $image_src=$url;
        }

        if (!$error)
        {
```

```
// create post content
$content='<a href="'.$image_url.'"><img src="'.
$image_src.'"></a><p>'.$description.'</p>';

// post information
$data = array
(
   'post_title' => $wpdb->escape($title),
   'post_content' => $wpdb->escape($content),
   'post_status' => $post_status
);

// insert post
$published_id = wp_insert_post($data);
// add a custom field
add_post_meta($published_id, "post-type",     __
('Photo',$this->plugin_domain)

if ($image_uploaded)
{
  $attachment = array
  (
     'post_mime_type' => $file['type'],
     'guid' => $image_url,
     'post_parent' => $published_id,
     'post_title' => $wpdb->escape($title),
     'post_content' => $wpdb->escape($description),
  );

  // insert post attachment
  $aid = wp_insert_attachment($attachment, $file
  ['file'], $published_id);

  // update metadata
  if ( !is_wp_error($aid) )
  {
    wp_update_attachment_metadata
    ( $aid, wp_generate_attachment_metadata
    ( $aid, $file['file'] ) );
  }
}

// clear all fields
$title=''; $url=''; $description='';
  }
}
else
```

```
                    $error=__('You need to enter a title and add a
                    photo.',$this->plugin_domain);
            }
            include( 'template/photo.php');
            break;

            endswitch;

    }
```

The above code enables functionality for checking uploads, handling the uploaded file, and adding it to the post. This means that you can now start creating photo posts:

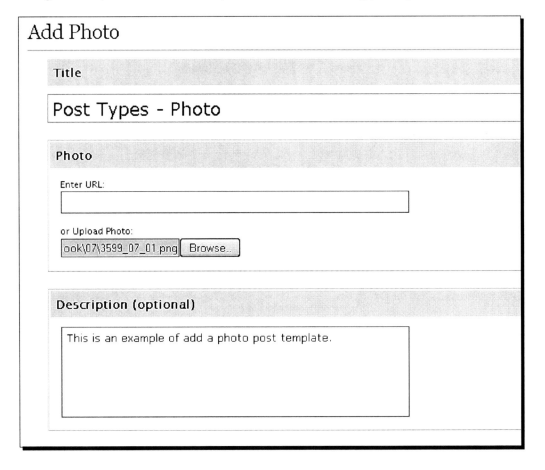

By doing this, the photo post will show up in your blog:

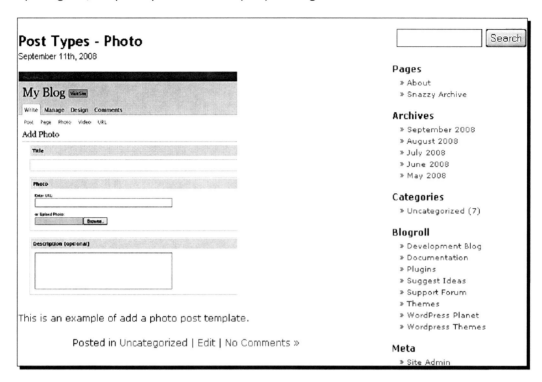

What just happened?

We have added support for uploading the files and also inserted the image to our post.

Let's analyze how this works.

First, we want to check if the `upload dir` is writeable. The location of the WordPress upload dir can be obtained by using the `wp_upload_dir()` function:

```
switch ($page) :

case 'add-photo':
// WordPress upload dir (wp-content/uploads)
$uploads = wp_upload_dir();
```

If the folder is writeable, we will show the file upload field on the form by setting the `$uploadfile` variable to true.

```
// WordPress upload dir (wp-content/uploads)
  $uploads = wp_upload_dir();
// check permissions
if (is_writable($uploads['path']))
{
  $uploadfile=true;
}
```

Now comes the part when we check if the post was published properly, and if there was an image uploaded with it.

The information about uploaded file(s) is stored in the global PHP `$_FILES` variable, and we are interested in the `upload` reference as that is the name of our upload file field.

```
$url=$_POST['url'];
$upload=$_FILES['upload'];

if ($published)
{
  if (!empty($title) && (!empty($upload['tmp_name']) || !empty($url)))
  {
    // if file uploaded
    if ($upload['tmp_name'])
    {
      // handle uploaded image
      $file=$this->handle_image_upload($upload);
```

The `handle_image_upload()` function uses another built-in WordPress function to check if the uploaded file—`file_is_displayable_image()`—is really an image.

```
function handle_image_upload($upload)
{
  // check if image
  if (file_is_displayable_image( $upload['tmp_name'] ))
  {
```

Further on, we call the `wp_handle_upload()` function. The purpose of this function is to check the uploaded file (type, size etc) and move it to the WordPress uploads folder.

You can specify certain overrides; in this case we are overriding the test for form action, as we are using a custom form.

```
if (file_is_displayable_image( $upload['tmp_name'] ))
{
  // handle the uploaded file
  $overrides = array('test_form' => false);
  $file=wp_handle_upload($upload, $overrides);
}
return $file;
}
```

The `wp_handle_upload()` function handles everything for our file, including moving it to the upload directory and setting correct permissions. So, we do not need to worry about it. It also returns a reference to the newly created file, which contains useful information such as the new filename and a URL to the file, which we will need for displaying the photo.

In the next piece of code back in the main function, we will create a thumbnail of the uploaded image to show it in the post and link it to the original picture.

Let's see how this is done:

```
if ($file)
{
  $image_url=$file['url'];
  // create a thumbnail
  $size='medium';
  $resized = image_make_intermediate_size( $file['file'],
  get_option("{$size}_size_w"), get_option("{$size}_size_h"),
  get_option("{$size}_crop") );

  if ($resized)
    $image_src=$uploads['url'] .'/'.$resized['file'];
  else
    $image_src=$image_url;

    $image_uploaded=true;
}
else
  $error=__('Please upload a valid image.',$this->plugin_domain);
}
```

We use the WordPress `image_make_intermediate_size()` function, which accepts the filename and resizing information as parameters. We chose to use the `medium` size, which is already defined in the WordPress backend; height and width are stored in the `medium_size_h` and `medium_size_w` options, respectively.

Settings for the upload folder (**Uploading**) and **Image sizes** can be found on the WordPress **Miscellaneous Settings** page:

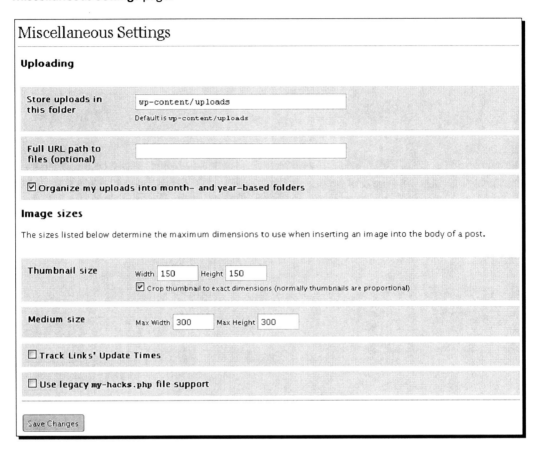

We also need to handle cases where the picture is specified by a URL, in which case we will just use the provided information:

```
    else
        $error=__('Please upload a valid image.',$this->plugin_domain);
    }
    else // if file uploaded
    {
        $image_url=$url;
        $image_src=$url;
    }
```

Now, when we have the picture information, we can create the post content and insert a new post:

```
// create post content
$content='<a href="'.$image_url.'"><img src="'.$image_src.'">
</a><p>'.$description.'</p>';
// post information
$data = array
(
    'post_title' => $wpdb->escape($title),
    'post_content' => $wpdb->escape($content),
    'post_status' => $post_status
);
// insert post
$published_id = wp_insert_post($data);
```

We will insert a `custom field` for our post, call it `post-type` and specify that it is a `Photo`.

```
// add a custom field
add_post_meta($published_id,
"post-type",__('Photo',$this->plugin_domain));
```

Custom fields allow us to insert any type of information to WordPress posts and pages, and in fact allow us transform WordPress into a CMS. We will get back to the custom fields in more detail later.

We have uploaded and processed the image. If we want to follow it up all the way, we want to add our photo to the WordPress Media Library by using the `wp_insert_attachment` function.

```
if ($image_uploaded)
{
  $attachment = array
  (
    'post_mime_type' => $file['type'],
    'guid' => $image_url,
    'post_parent' => $published_id,
    'post_title' => $wpdb->escape($title),
    'post_content' => $wpdb->escape($description),
  );
  // insert post attachment
  $aid = wp_insert_attachment($attachment, $file['file'],
  $published_id);
  // update metadata
```

```
if ( !is_wp_error($aid) )
{
  wp_update_attachment_metadata( $aid,
  wp_generate_attachment_metadata( $aid, $file['file'] ) );
}
```

After we have done this, all new photos will turn up in the in the WordPress Media Library (**Manage Media**) looking like this:

Quick reference

`wp_handle_upload(&$file, $overrides)`: A function which handles user uploaded files. Takes information provided by the `$_FILES[]` variable and the desired overrides (`test_form`, `test_type`, `test_size`).

`file_is_displayable_image($file)`: It checks if the file is an image that WordPress can display.

`wp_upload_dir()`: A function which returns the path to the WordPress uploads folder.

`image_make_intermediate_size($file, $width, $height, $crop=false)`: A function which resizes the image and returns the new file metadata.

`add_post_meta($post_id, $meta_key, $meta_value, $unique)`: The function used to add a custom field to the specified post. The field is identified with a key (`$meta_key`) and its value (`$meta_value`).

`wp_insert_attachment($attachment, $filename, $parent_post_id)`: This function inserts an attachment for a post, into the Media Library. More information can be found at: `http://codex.wordpress.org/Function_Reference/wp_insert_attachment`

`wp_update_attachment_metadata($post_id, $data)`: This function updates attachment metadata, usually used in conjunction with `wp_generate_attachment_metadata`.

`wp_generate_attachment_metadata($attachment_id, $file)`: This function generates the post Image attachment Metadata.

Using custom fields

Custom fields are used in WordPress to store additional information about a post. They are normally available to you in the **Write Post** screen as **Key/Value** pairs.

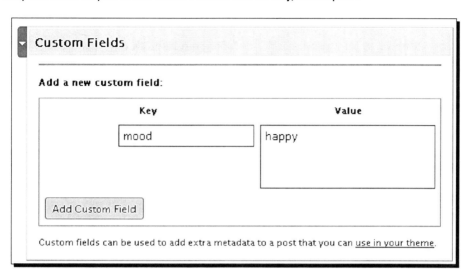

You can use custom fields to display information on the site or for some other kind of special processing (like storing a post's expiration date).

Adding custom fields

To add a custom field from the code, you can use the add_post_meta() function:

```
add_post_meta($post_id, $meta_key, $meta_value, $unique)
```

- ◆ post_id: This parameter contains the ID of the post where the custom field is to be added.
- ◆ meta_key: This parameter contains the key identifier (such as mood, job-type).
- ◆ meta_value: This parameter contains the value for the key (such as happy, temporarily, and so on).
- ◆ unique: This parameter contains is used to decide whether you want this key to be unique. WordPress supports multiple values for the same key, and if the value set is unique, only one instance for the given key is allowed.prev_value: This contains the previous value of the key, which helps us to differentiate the values if the key is not unique.

To update existing fields, you can use the update_post_meta() function:

```
update_post_meta($post_id, $meta_key, $meta_value, $prev_value)
```

Retrieving custom fields

To retrieve custom fields, you can use one of the following functions:

`get_post_custom($post_id)`: This function returns a multidimensional array with all the custom fields of a particular post or page.

`get_post_custom_keys($post_id)`: This function returns an array containing the keys of all custom fields of a particular post or page.

`get_post_custom_values($key, $post_id)`: This function gets the list of values for a particular key on the current post.

`get_post_meta($post_id, $key, $single = false)`: This function gets the value for the specified key in a given post. If `$single` is `true`, then only the first key is returned (even if there are more).

For example:

```
get_post_meta(223, 'mood', false);
```

Quick reference

More on Custom Fields – `http://codex.wordpress.org/Using_Custom_Fields`

Quick post a link

Adding the link post type is easy when we know how to display the form and handle it. So, let's quickly add the link template to our plugin:

Time for action – Add link template

1. Lets create `template/link.php` file

```
<div class="wrap">

    <?php    if (!empty($error)) : ?>
       <div id="message" class="error fade">
         <p><?php echo $error; ?></p>
       </div>
    <?php    elseif (!empty($published_id)) : ?>
       <div id="message" class="updated fade">
         <p><strong><?php _e('Link added.',$this->plugin_domain);
    ?>
```

```
        </strong> <a href="<?php echo get_permalink(
                                   $published_id);
        ?>"><?php _e('View post',$this->plugin_domain); ?>
        &raquo;</a></p>
    </div>
<?php endif; ?>


<h2><?php _e('Add Link',$this->plugin_domain); ?></h2>
<form action="" method="post">
<?php wp_nonce_field($_GET['page']); ?>

    <div id="poststuff">

    <div class="submitbox" id="submitpost">
    <div id="previewview"></div>
    <div class="inside"></div>
      <p class="submit"><input name="publish" type="submit"
      class="button button-highlighted" tabindex="4" value="<?php
      _e\('Publish', $this->plugin_domain);  ?>" /></p>
    </div>

    <div id="post-body">

    <div id="titlediv">
      <h3><?php _e('Title (optional)',$this->plugin_domain); ?>
      </h3>
    <div id="titlewrap"><input type="text" name="title" tabindex=
    "1" value="<?php echo $title; ?>" id="title" /></div>
    </div>

    <div class="postbox ">
      <h3><?php _e('URL',$this->plugin_domain); ?></h3>
    <div class="inside">
      <p>
        <input style="width: 415px" type="text" tabindex="2"
        name="url" id="url" value="<?php echo $url ?>" />
      </p>
    </div>
    </div>

    <div class="postbox ">
      <h3><?php _e('Description (optional)',
      $this->plugin_domain); ?></h3>
    <div class="inside">
      <textarea name="description" id="description" rows="5"
      style="width: 415px" tabindex="3"><?php echo $description ?>
      </textarea>
```

```
            </div>
            </div>

            </div>
            </div>
        </form>
    </div>
```

2. Then, add a new submenu page for the Write screen :

```
// Hook the admin menu
function admin_menu()
{

  // submenu pages
  add_submenu_page('post-new.php', __('Add Photo',$this-
  >plugin_domain) , __('Photo', $this->plugin_domain) , 1
  , 'add-photo',  array(&$this, 'display_form') );
  add_submenu_page('post-new.php', __('Add URL', $this-
  >plugin_domain) ,  __('URL', $this->plugin_domain)    , 1 ,
  'add-url',  array(&$this, 'display_form') );
}
```

3. And finally, add the code to the `display_form()` switch/case to handle the rendering of the link form:

```
    include( 'template/photo.php');
    break;

    case 'add-url':
    $url=$_POST['url'];

    if ($published)
    {
      if (!empty($url))
      {
        if (empty($title))
        $title=$url;

        $content='<a href="'.$url.'">'.$title.'</a>
        <p>'.$description.'</p>';
        $data = array
        (
          'post_title' => $wpdb->escape($title),
          'post_content' => $wpdb->escape($content),
          'post_status' => $post_status
        );
        // insert post
        $published_id = wp_insert_post($data);
```

```
        // add a custom field
        add_post_meta($published_id, "post-type", __
        ('Link',$this->plugin_domain));
        // clear all fields
        $title=''; $url=''; $description='';
      }
      else
        $error=__ ('You need to enter a URL.',$this->plugin_domain);
    }
    include( 'template/link.php');
    break;
  endswitch;
```

With that done, we now have a second post-type ready:

What just happened?

We have added another post template using the previous form as a starting point. The code is very similar, so we will not go into the details.

The recipe for adding further forms is:

- Create a new form based on a previous one and edit the form fields.

- Add the submenu page in the `admin_menu()` function.

- Add the form-specific handling code in the switch/case of `display_form()`.

You can add as many forms as you like, for example to enter simple text, video, a quote, and so on.

Tinkering with WordPress backend menus

Since we added the **URL** page under the **Write** menu, and there is already a **Link** page there (for adding links to the blogroll), we would like to remove the **Link** page from the menus to prevent confusion.

You can easily do this (in fact, you can totally rearrange WordPress menus in any way you like).

Time for action - Remove 'Link' from the Write page

1. Removing an item from a menu is a simple matter. Lets add this code to the `admin_menu()` function:

```
// Hook to admin menu
    function admin_menu()
    {
        global $submenu;

        // remove 'Link' from Write menu
        unset($submenu['post-new.php'][15]);

        // submenu pages
        add_submenu_page('post-new.php', __('Add Photo',$this-
        >plugin_domain) , __('Photo', $this->plugin_domain) , 1 ,
        'add-photo',  array(&$this, 'display_form') );
```

2. That's all! The link page no longer shows in the menu.

What just happened?

We removed the **Link** page from the menus by unsetting it from the submenu array.

WordPress holds the entire backend menu structure in two globally available variables $menu and $submenu.

Using these two variables, not only can you read entries, you can also change and delete entries in the menus, and customize the menu structure to your liking by simply editing the arrays.

To do that, we must first learn what this structure looks like. The easiest way to do that is to use the print_r() function to dump the variable in a readable form.

Here is the sample output of print_r($menu):

```
Array
(
  [0] => Array
    (
        [0] => Dashboard
        [1] => read
        [2] => index.php
    )
  [5] => Array
    (
        [0] => Write
        [1] => edit_posts
        [2] => post-new.php
    )
  [10] => Array
    (
        [0] => Manage
        [1] => edit_posts
        [2] => edit.php
    )
```

```
    [15] => Array
       (
          [0] => Design
          [1] => switch_themes
          [2] => themes.php
       )
    [20] => Array
       (
          [0] => Comments <span id='awaiting-mod' class='count-0'>
                <span class='comment-count'>0</span></span>
          [1] => edit_posts
          [2] => edit-comments.php
       )
```

As you can see, the menus are organized into multidimensional arrays. If you remove elements of this array, they will not be displayed in the menu anymore.

For example:

```
unset($menu[10]); // Remove Manage Menu
unset($menu[15]); // Remove Design Menu
unset($menu[20]); // Remove Comments Menu
```

This piece of code will cause the **Manage**, **Design,** and **Comments** pages to disappear from the WordPress main menu leaving with only the with **Write** menu:

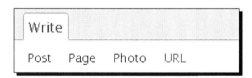

Similarly, we remove the **Link** page from the submenus:

```
// remove 'Link' from Write menu
unset($submenu['post-new.php'][15]);
```

Using the menu arrays, you can customize the backend of a WordPress site to show only relevant information for your purpose. If you are turning WordPress into a CMS, implementing custom fields and tinkering with menus would be the first things on the list.

We can also hack into the **Manage** panel, which will allow us to show custom information in the post listings. Let's learn how to do that!

Programming the Manage panel

The **Manage Posts** screen can be changed to show extra columns, or remove unwanted columns in the listing.

Let's say that we want to show the post type—Normal, Photo or Link. Remember the custom field post-type that we added to our posts? We can use it now to differentiate post types.

Time for action – Add post type column in the Manage panel

We want to add a new column to the **Manage** panel, and we will call it **Type**. The value of the column will represent the post type—**Normal**, **Photo** or **Link**.

1. Expand the admin_menu() function to load the function to handle **Manage Page hooks**:

```
add_submenu_page('post-new.php', __('Add URL',
$this->plugin_domain) ,  __('URL', $this->plugin_domain) , 1 ,
'add-url', array(&$this, 'display_form') );
// handle Manage page hooks
add_action('load-edit.php', array(&$this, 'handle_load_edit') );
}
```

2. Add the hooks to the columns on the Manage screen:

```
// Manage page hooks
function handle_load_edit()
{
    // handle Manage screen functions
    add_filter('manage_posts_columns', array(&$this,
    'handle_posts_columns'));
    add_action('manage_posts_custom_column', array(&$this,
    'handle_posts_custom_column'), 10, 2);
}
```

3. Then implement the function to add a new Column, remove the author and replace the date with our date format :

```
// Handle Column header
function handle_posts_columns($columns)
{
    // add 'type' column
    $columns['type'] = __('Type',$this->plugin_domain);
    return $columns;
}
```

4. For date key replacement, we need an extra function:

```
function array_change_key_name( $orig, $new, &$array )
{
  foreach ( $array as $k => $v )
  $return[ ( $k === $orig ) ? $new : $k ] = $v;
  return ( array ) $return;
}
```

5. And finally, insert a function to handle the display of information in that column:

```
// Handle Type column display
function handle_posts_custom_column($column_name, $id)
{
    // 'type' column handling based on post type
    if( $column_name == 'type' )
    {
        $type=get_post_meta($id, 'post-type', true);
        echo $type ? $type : __('Normal',$this->plugin_domain);
    }
}
```

6. Don't forget to add the manage page to the list of localized pages:

```
// pages where our plugin needs translation
$local_pages=array('plugins.php', 'post-new.php', 'edit.php');

if (in_array($pagenow, $local_pages))
```

As a result, we now have a new column that displays the post type using information from a post custom field.

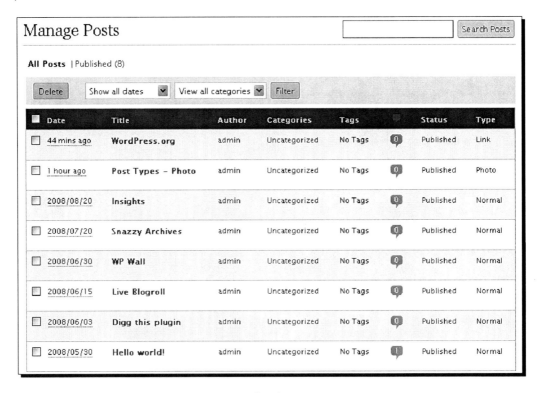

What just happened?

We have used the `load-edit.php` action to specify that we want our hooks to be assigned only on the **Manage Posts** page (`edit.php`). This is similar to the optimization we did when we loaded the localization files.

The `handle_posts_columns` is a filter that accepts the columns as a parameter and allows you to insert a new column:

```
function handle_posts_columns($columns)
{
  $columns['type'] = __('Type',$this->plugin_domain);
  return $columns;
}
```

You are also able to remove a column. This example would remove the **Author** column:

```
unset($columns['author']);
```

To handle information display in that column, we use the `handle_posts_custom_column` action.

The action is called for each entry (post), whenever an unknown column is encountered. WordPress passes the name of the column and current post ID as parameters.

That allows us to extract the post type from a custom field:

```
function handle_posts_custom_column($column_name, $id)
{
  if( $column_name == 'type' )
  {
    $type=get_post_meta($id, 'post-type', true);
```

It also allows us to print it out:

```
    echo $type ? $type : __('Normal',$this->plugin_domain);
  }
}
```

Modifying an existing column

We can also modify an existing column. Let's say we want to change the way **Date** is displayed.

Here are the changes we would make to the code:

```
// Handle Column header
function handle_posts_columns($columns)
{
```

```
        // add 'type' column
        $columns['type'] = __('Type',$this->plugin_domain);

        // remove 'author' column
        //unset($columns['author']);

        // change 'date' column
        $columns = $this->array_change_key_name( 'date', 'date_new',
        $columns );

        return $columns;
    }
    // Handle Type column display
    function handle_posts_custom_column($column_name, $id)
    {
        // 'type' column handling based on post type
        if( $column_name == 'type' )
        {
            $type=get_post_meta($id, 'post-type', true);
            echo $type ? $type : __('Normal',$this->plugin_domain);
        }
        // new date column handling
    if( $column_name == 'date_new' )
    {
        the_time('Y-m-d <br \> g:i:s a');
    }
    }
function array_change_key_name( $orig, $new, &$array )
{
    foreach ( $array as $k => $v )
    $return[ ( $k === $orig ) ? $new : $k ] = $v;
    return ( array ) $return;
}
```

The example replaces the date column with our own date_new column and uses it to display the date with our preferred formatting.

Manage screen search filter

WordPress allows us to show all the posts by date and category, but what if we want to show all the posts depending on post type?

No problem! We can add a new filter select box straight to the **Manage** panel.

Time for action – Add a search filter box

1. Let's start by adding two more hooks to the `handle_load_edit()` function. The `restrict_manage_posts` function draws the search box and the `posts_where` alters the database query to select only the posts of the type we want to show.

```
// Manage page hooks
function handle_load_edit()
{
    // handle Manage screen functions
    add_filter('manage_posts_columns',
    array(&$this, 'handle_posts_columns'));
    add_action('manage_posts_custom_column',
    array(&$this, 'handle_posts_custom_column'), 10, 2);

    // handle search box filter
    add_filter('posts_where',
    array(&$this, 'handle_posts_where'));
    add_action('restrict_manage_posts',
    array(&$this, 'handle_restrict_manage_posts'));
}
```

2. Let's write the corresponding function to draw the select box:

```
// Handle select box for Manage page
function handle_restrict_manage_posts()
{
  ?>
  <select name="post_type" id="post_type" class="postform">
  <option value="0">View all types</option>
  <option value="normal" <?php if ( $_GET['post_type']=='normal')
  echo 'selected="selected"' ?>><?php _e
  ('Normal',$this->plugin_domain); ?></option>
  <option value="photo" <?php if ( $_GET['post_type']=='photo')
  echo 'selected="selected"' ?>><?php _e
  ('Photo',$this->plugin_domain); ?></option>
```

```
        <option value="link" <?php if ( $_GET['post_type']=='link')
        echo 'selected="selected"' ?>><?php _e
        ('Link',$this->plugin_domain); ?></option>
        </select>
        <?php
    }
```

3. And finally, we need a function that will change the query to retrieve only the posts of the selected type:

```
// Handle query for Manage page
function handle_posts_where($where)
{
    global $wpdb;
    if( $_GET['post_type'] == 'photo' )
    {
        $where .= " AND ID IN (SELECT post_id FROM {$wpdb->postmeta}
        WHERE meta_key='post-type' AND meta_value='".__
        ('Photo',$this->plugin_domain)."' )";
    }
    else if( $_GET['post_type'] == 'link' )
    {
        $where .= " AND ID IN (SELECT post_id FROM {$wpdb->postmeta}
        WHERE meta_key='post-type' AND meta_value='".__
        ('Link',$this->plugin_domain)."' )";
    }
    else if( $_GET['post_type'] == 'normal' )
    {
        $where .= " AND ID NOT IN (SELECT post_id FROM
        {$wpdb->postmeta} WHERE meta_key='post-type' )";
    }
    return $where;
}
```

What just happened?

We have added a new select box to the header of the **Manage** panel. It allows us to filter the post types we want to show.

We added the box using the restrict_manage_posts action that is triggered at the end of the **Manage** panel header and allows us to insert HTML code, which we used to draw a select box.

To actually perform the filtering, we use the `posts_where` filter, which is run when a query is made to fetch the posts from the database.

```
if ( $_GET['post_type'] == 'photo' )
{
  $where .= " AND ID IN (SELECT post_id FROM {$wpdb->postmeta}
  WHERE meta_key='post-type' AND meta_value='".__
  ('Photo',$this->plugin_domain)."' )";
```

If a photo is selected, we inspect the WordPress database `postmeta` table and select posts that have the `post-type` key with the value, `Photo`.

At this point, we have a functional plugin. What we can do further to improve it is to add user permissions checks, so that only those users allowed to write posts and upload files are allowed to use it.

Quick reference

`manage_posts_columns($columns)`: This acts as a filter for adding/ removing columns in the **Manage Posts** panel. Simlarly, we use the function, `manage_pages_columns` for the **Manage Pages** panel.

`manage_posts_custom_column($column, $post_id)`: This acts as an action to display information for the given column and post. Alternatively, `manage_pages_custom_column` for Manage Pages panel.

`posts_where($where)`: This acts as a filter for the `where` clause in the query that gets the posts.

`restrict_manage_posts`: This acts as an action that runs at the end of the **Manage** panel header and allows you to insert HTML.

Handling error messages

WordPress provides a simple class called `WP_Error` that allows us to keep all our error messages tidy and in one place.

Time for action – Adding support for errors

1. Change the plugin constructor to add initialization of error class:

```
if (version_compare($wp_version,"2.5","<"))
{
    exit ($exit_msg);
}

// initialize the error class
```

```
$this->error = new WP_Error();
$this->init_errors();

// add admin_menu action
add_action('admin_menu',  array(&$this, 'admin_menu'));
```

2. Initialize all our errors by defining the error code and the message:

```
// Init error messages
function init_errors()
{
    $this->error->add('e_image', __('Please upload a valid
    image.',$this->plugin_domain));
    $this->error->add('e_title', __('You need to enter a title
    and add a photo.',$this->plugin_domain));
    $this->error->add('e_url', __('You need to enter a
    URL.',$this->plugin_domain));
}
```

3. Add a function to retrieve an error:

```
//  Retrieve an error message
function my_error($e = '')
{
    $msg = $this->error->get_error_message($e);

    if ($msg == null)
    {
        return __("Unknown error occured, please contact the
        administrator.", $this->plugin_domain);
    }
    return $msg;
}
```

4. Finally replace the old error messages with our new function:

```
        else
        $error=$this->my_error('e_image');
    }
    else // if file uploaded
    else
        $error=$this->my_error('e_title');
    }
    include( 'template/photo.php');
    else
```

```
            $error=$this->my_error('e_url');
    }
    include( 'template/link.php');
```

What just happened?

We used the integrated WordPress error class for displaying error messages.

We initialize the class in the plugin constructor and call the error message initialization function:

```
$this->error = new WP_Error();
$this->init_errors();
```

To add new errors, we use the add method of the error class, and define the message with code and text:

```
$this->error->add('e_image', __('Please upload a valid
image.',$this->plugin_domain));
```

We then created the my_error function that retrieves the error message using the get_error_message method:

```
$msg = $this->error->get_error_message($e);
```

Quick reference

WP_Error: This is the WordPress class for handling error messages. Use the add and get_error_message methods to store and retrieve messages.

User roles and capabilities

Let's add some checks to our plugin to prevent unauthorized users from publishing posts and uploading files using our post templates.

This can be done using the WordPress capabilities system, providing us with functions to check if the user is allowed to perform a certain action.

Time for action – Add user capability checks

1. Let's add our first check, to see if the user can publish posts. All capability checks are performed using the `current_user_can()` function.

   We will include a new variable in the `display_form()` function to hold the new post's status:

   ```
   if ($published)
   {
     check_admin_referer($page);
     $post_status = current_user_can('publish_posts') ?
     'publish' : 'pending';
   }
   ```

2. Change the **Publish** button in both the template files, `link.php` and `photo.php`, to show different text if the user can not publish:

   ```
   <div class="submitbox" id="submitpost">
     <div id="previewview"></div>
     <div class="inside"></div>
   <p class="submit"><input name="publish" type="submit"
   class="button button-highlighted" tabindex="4"
   value="<?php if (current_user_can('publish_posts'))
   _e('Publish', $this->plugin_domain); else _e('Submit',
   $this->plugin_domain); ?>" /></p>
     </div>
   ```

3. Finally, edit the `display_form(` to check if the current user is allowed to upload files:

   ```
       // check permissions
   if (is_writable($uploads['path']) &&
   current_user_can('upload_files'))
       {
           $uploadfile=true;
       }
   ```

With the capabilities systems in place, we are now able to restrict the actions of users without enough privileges to publish the post or upload files to the server.

Congratulations! That was the last bit of code needed to finish our last plugin!

What just happened?

User capabilities provide a flexible model for checking the permissions of the user.

Roles and capabilities are interconnected, but the capabilities of a role can be changed dynamically by other plugins. So it is adviseable to always check for capabilities instead of roles.

User capabilities are checked using the `current_user_can($action)` function, which accepts the desired action as a parameter. Actions can be `edit_posts`, or `upload_plugins`, and so on.

Bearing in mind that WordPress sites can be used by multiple users, you should always make sure to assign the correct capabilities for the features of you plugin.

Quick reference

`current_user_can($action)`: This function is used to check if the current user is capable of performing a certain action.

A full reference for roles and capabilities is available at `http://codex.wordpress.org/Roles_and_Capabilities`.

Have a go Hero

With this plugin, we explored the core of the WordPress backend.

There are a few features you can consider now, that could improve this plugin further:

- Include tags and perhaps categories to the post templates
- Create more interesting post templates
- For the `photo` template, you can download the image instead of linking to it, if the image is specified with a URL
- Create a mobile phone friendly admin panel by removing all other unnecessary menus and leaving only the quick post templates

Summary

The purpose of the Post Types plugin was to introduce you to different aspects of WordPress backend development.

While creating our different post types, we have learned how to customize WordPress menus to our liking. We used custom fields to insert important information to the post which we do not want to be visible in the post content.

We learned how to modify the **Manage Posts** panel to display the information we want. We also covered user capabilities, and how using them, we can make sure our plugin is working in multi-user environments.

Finally, we do not want to forget localization, for there are thousands of users who use WordPress in their native language.

Here are the most important lessons from this chapter:

- **Localization**: Not everyone uses WordPress in English
- **Backend CSS classes**: Use them to make your forms prettier
- **Custom fields**: They are the powerhouse behind WordPress CMS capabilities
- **Customize Menus**: Your plugin can choose the menus in the WordPress backend
- **Manage Panels**: Customize the display of information to your liking, using custom columns and filters
- **Manage Errors**: Use the WordPress `WP_Error` class to handle errors in your plugin
- **User capabilities**: Use this to restrict access to functions for users without the relevant permissions

We have one more exciting chapter to go, with useful advice on how to distribute and promote your plugin, and other more advanced tips.

8
Development Goodies

Plugin development does not end with a finished plugin—depending on the plugin's purpose there are several more phases a plugin author needs to consider.

This chapter will cover additional steps involved in localizing, documenting, publishing, and promoting the plugin. It will also cover useful tips and ideas to further improve your general WordPress knowledge.

In this chapter, you will learn about:

- ◆ Handling localization files
- ◆ Managing documentation and providing support
- ◆ Managing your plugin using SVN and publishing it to the WordPress Plugin Repository
- ◆ Distributing and promoting your plugin
- ◆ Staying up-to-date by working on the latest development version of WordPress

The final sections of the chapter are devoted to information about WordPress MU development and other useful online resources.

Creating Localization files

In Chapter 7, we have learned how to use the localization functionalities provided by WordPress. Using the __() and _e() functions, we can specify localizable text that users can translate to different languages.

We can split the localization process in two phases.

In the first phase, you need to generate a POT file that will describe all localizable strings used in the plugin.

In the second phase, users generate `.po` and `.mo` files in their desired language. A PO file is the same as a POT file, but includes translated strings in another language. A MO file is actually a compiled PO file and is loaded by the `load_text_domain()` function that we used in the WordPress plugin.

Localization process is usually performed using external tools that are available for Windows, Mac OS or Linux platforms. Example of one such popular multi-platform tool is Poedit, which we will use in this chapter.

Time for action - Create a POT file

Here is how to create a `.pot` file using Poedit:

1. If you do not have it already, download Poedit from
   `http://www.poedit.net/download.php`

2. Select the option **New catalog...** under the **File** menu. It will open a window where you can fill in some basic details, including your plugin name. You may also want to fill in the default plugin language and the file charset:

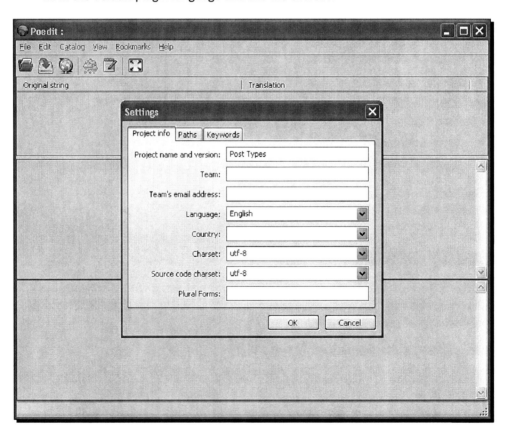

3. In the **Paths** tab, add **../** for the base path as we will keep the language files inside the lang/ folder in the plugin.

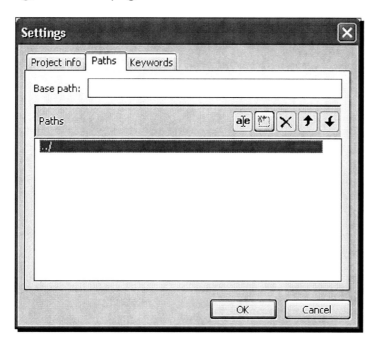

4. Finally, in the **Keywords** tab, add **__** and **_e** as our language functions.

5. Press **OK** and then select **All files** from the **Save** dialog. Save the file in the `lang/` folder of the plugin, manually typing `.pot` as the extension.

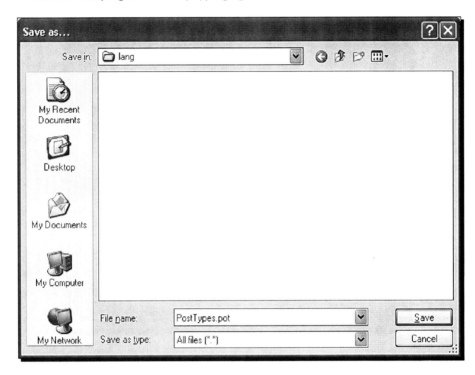

6. After the file is saved, Poedit will scan through your plugin files and display a list of all the strings that can be translated.

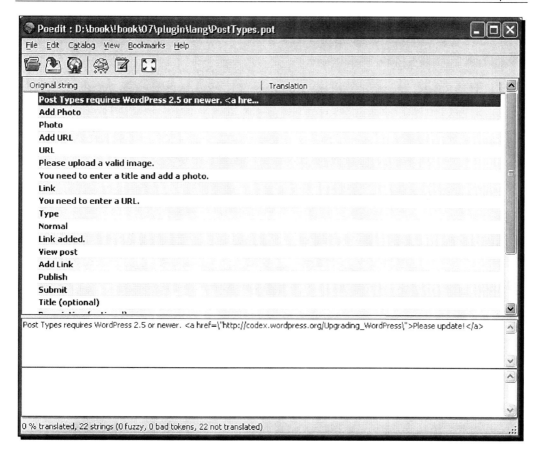

What just happened?

You have created basic a POT file that users can use to create translations in their own language.

Updating POT file

You will need to update the POT file manually with every new release of your plugin. To do this, you need to do the following:

1. Open the POT file.

2. Select the **Update from sources** option from the **Catalog** menu.

3. Save the POT file.

Time for action – Perform translation

Here is how to create a new translation:

1. Start Poedit, and select **New catalog from POT file...** from the **File** menu.

2. Select the POT file supplied with the plugin. Now, you can enter the project information relating to the translation.

3. Go through all the strings and translate them. Be careful to leave all the %s and %d references. These will be replaced with a string or a number by the plugin.

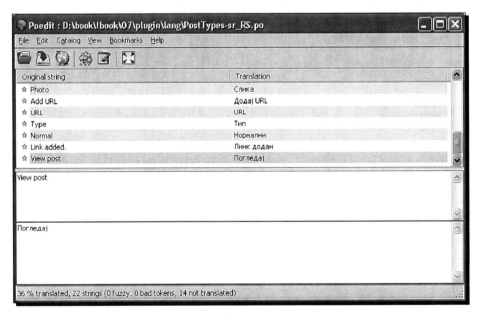

When you are done, you need to save the PO file. The usual practice is to use the POT filename and a language code. If our POT file was `PostTypes.pot`, we would name, for example, the Serbian translation (language code `sr_RS`) of the file, `PostTypes-sr_RS.po`. When you save the PO file, the MO file will be automatically generated.

What just happened?

We have created a language translation file that our plugin can automatically use when it detects a WordPress blog in that language.

You will notice that we use the language code. This matches the installation language of WordPress and is retrieved using the `get_locale()` function in our WordPress plugin.

Some of these codes are:

- `fr_FR`: French
- `de_DE`: German
- `es_ES`: Spanish
- `zh_CN`: Chinese

You can view the list of all the language codes at theWordPress Codex page `http://codex.wordpress.org/WordPress_in_Your_Language`.

Updating translation

When a new version of the plugin is released, the translation file needs to be updated. To do that, you can follow these steps:

1. Using Poedit, open your translated PO file (for example `PostTypes-sr_RS.po`).
2. Select the **Update from POT file...** option in the **Catalog** menu. Now select the POT file that had previously been updated to a new version.
3. Poedit will show you what is new, and what is not used anymore.
4. When you are done translating, save the PO file again.

Normally, if you supply the POT file with your plugin, users will start sending you the translations. It is a good practice to mention and thank these users in your plugin credits sections.

Quick reference

Translating WordPress: `http://codex.wordpress.org/ Translating_WordPress`

WordPress in your language (and list of all language codes): `http://codex. wordpress.org/WordPress_in_Your_Language`

Poedit: `http://www.poedit.net`

Documentation and support

Creating documentation for your plugin is a crucial step, especially if you are developing a plugin for public release.

Some plugin authors, in a hurry to release their plugin, may choose to skip this step, resulting in poor or inadequately prepared 'readme' files. This is bad practice because usually the success of the plugin greatly depends on the available documentation.

Plugin readme file

To prepare documentation for the public release of a plugin, you need to complete two steps.

1. Create a plugin `readme.txt` file.

2. Prepare a page on your site (if you do not have a site you can use the WordPress plugin repository instead—we will discuss this later).

The `readme.txt` file is a standardized text file describing the plugin functionality, installation and usage manual.

The contents of a `readme.txt` file are automatically parsed by the WordPress plugin repository to display a plugin information page that looks like this one:

Insights

Description Installation Faq Screenshots Other Notes Stats

Admin

Author: Vladimir Prelovac

Insights brings a **powerful** new way to write your blog posts. It increases **productivity** and at the same time **quality of your posts**.

Insights performs following functions in **real-time**:

- Interlink your posts
- Insert Flickr images
- Insert Youtube videos
- Search Wikipedia
- Search Google
- Insert a Google Map

Check the **screenshots** for more examples of usage.

Insights allows you to do all this using dynamic AJAX interface which loads the relevant information to your post in just a few seconds.

Tags: Post, media, play, video, youtube, jquery, AJAX, google, links, images, posts, admin

Download

FYI

Version: 0.3.1
Other Versions ››
Last Updated: 2008-9-25
Requires WordPress Version: 2.3
  or higher
Compatible up to: 2.6.2
Author Homepage ››
Plugin Homepage ››
Donate to this plugin ››

Average Rating   Your Rating

☆☆☆☆☆ ☆☆☆☆☆
(5 ratings)

See what others are saying...

1. **[New Plugin: Insights]**

Got something to say? Need help?
Write a new topic.

Time for action – Create a sample plugin readme.txt file

Let's create an example `readme.txt` file for the Insights plugin.

1. First comes the general information section. This section contains general information on the plugin such as the name, author, tags, version information and a donation link.

```
=== Insights ===
Contributors: freediver
Donate link: https://www.networkforgood.org/donation/MakeDonation.
    aspx?ORGID2=520781390
Tags:  admin, posts, images, links, google, ajax, jquery, youtube,
    video, play, media, Post, posts
Requires at least: 2.3
Tested up to: 2.6.2
Stable tag: trunk

Insights allows you to quickly access and insert information
    (links, images, videos, maps..) into your blog posts.
```

2. Then, we have the plugin description:

```
== Description ==
```

Insights brings a **powerful** new way to write your blog posts. It increases **productivity** and at the same time **quality of your posts**.

Insights perform following functions in **real-time**:

```
* Interlink your posts
* Insert Flickr images
* Insert Youtube videos
* Search Wikipedia
* Search Google
* Insert a Google Map
```

Check the [screenshots](http://wordpress.org/extend/plugins/insights/screenshots/) for more examples of usage.

Insights allows you to do all this using dynamic AJAX interface which loads the relevant information to your post in just a few seconds.

3. Next, we have the installation and usage instructions:

```
== Installation ==
```

1. Upload the whole plugin folder to your /wp-content/ plugins/ folder.
2. Go to the 'Plugins' page in the menu and activate the plugin.
3. Use the 'Options' page to change your plugin options.
4. If you want to use Google Maps module then get your free Google Maps key here: http://code.google.com/apis/maps/signup.html
5. Write a new post. You will notice Insights toolbar. Use it :)

4. The screenshots section describes your screenshots. It makes your plugin presentation look much better:

```
== Screenshots ==
```

1. Searching images on Flickr and adding them
2. Searching Youtube videos, add to post
3. Adding a Google Map!
4. Using Wikipedia
5. Searching my Blog and linking to a post

5. These sections can be followed by optional Credits, License and FAQ sections:

```
== Credits ==

The ideas for a quickly accessible Google Maps solution came from
[Ubiquity](http://labs.mozilla.com/projects/ubiquity/) plugin for
Firefox, which is just pure coolness.

Thanks.

== License ==

This file is part of Insights.

Insights is free software: you can redistribute it and/or modify
it under the terms of the GNU General Public License as published
by the Free Software Foundation, either version 3 of the License,
or (at your option) any later version.

Insights is distributed in the hope that it will be useful,
but WITHOUT ANY WARRANTY; without even the implied warranty of
MERCHANTABILITY or FITNESS FOR A PARTICULAR PURPOSE. See the GNU
General Public License for more details.

You should have received a copy of the GNU General Public License
along with Insights. If not, see <http://www.gnu.org/licenses/>.

== Frequently Asked Questions ==

= Can I suggest a feature for the plugin? =

Of course, visit [Insights Home Page](http://www.prelovac.com/
vladimir/wordpress-plugins/Insights#comments)
```

What just happened?

We have created a properly formed `readme.txt` file for the plugin, which not only helps the users who downloaded your plugin, but is also required if you want to host your plugin at the WordPress plugin repository.

Sections of readme.txt

The readme file can contain several sections encapsulated in the `==` characters. These sections are recognized by the plugin repository and are used for creating sections on the plugin information page automatically. The sections are:

- Plugin name and information
- Description
- Installation
- Credits
- Screenshot

- License
- Frequently Asked Questions
- Any arbitrary section, these will be displayed after the recognized sections

General information

The first section is used to describe general plugin information. It contains important data about the plugin:

- **Contributors**: This shows the user names of authors in the repository
- **Donate link**: This can be used used for collecting donations for your work
- **Tags**: It is a list of descriptive tags about your plugin
- **Requires at least**: Displays the minimum WordPress version required
- **Tested up to**: Indicates the latest version of WordPress with which the plugin has been tested
- **Stable tag**: SVN tag are used for the stable version; use of trunk (will be explained later)

Special codes

The plugin repository allows you to use several special codes in the readme file text. They are:

- For highlighting text, you could place it between wildcards (example 'this is *important*') or double wildcards ('this is **very important**')
- If you want to create a list, use a wildcard at the beginning of each new line. Example:

  ```
  * Item 1
  * Item 2
  ```

- To create links, use the [link text](link URL) format. For example: [WordPress](http://www.wordpress.org)

Screenshots

The repository also searches for files named `screenshot-1.png, screenshot-2.png` in your plugin root folder and displays them in the **Screenshots** section.

To add descriptions for the screenshots, simply create a list in the `Screenshots` sections of the readme file.

```
== Screenshots ==
1. Searching images on Flickr and adding them
```

```
2. Searching Youtube videos, add to post
3. Adding a Google Map!
4. Using Wikipedia
5. Searching my Blog and linking to a post
```

Installation instructions

The installation section should contain the information necessary to install and run the plugin. Consider updating your installation section as you become aware of the problems your users may be experiencing.

Even if the plugin is simple, this section should still have basic installation instructions such as:

```
1. Upload the whole plugin folder to your /wp-content/plugins/ folder.
2. Go to the 'Plugins' page in the menu and activate the plugin.
3. Use the 'Options' page to change your plugin options.
```

Keeping the installation and usage instructions up-to-date will save you a lot of time in addressing support questions!

Quick reference

readme.txt template: http://wordpress.org/extend/plugins/about/readme.txt

Readme validator: Use this to validate your readme file before submitting. http://wordpress.org/extend/plugins/about/validator/

Plugin homepage

The plugin page is an important part of promoting your plugin as well as giving the users necessary information. This is the page you would usually link from the plugin header. You should make sure it is descriptive and well written. If you've made good effort to prepare the readme.txt file, you will find it much easier to create this page.

You can usually copy over most of the text from the readme file, and you will have all the screenshots ready for uploading to your post.

Useful plugin page tips

Include the large Download link or button, and make it visible immediately. Many users will come to the plugin page simply to download it.

It would be good if the download link pointed to the file in the WordPress repository.

If your plugin needs explicit installation and usage instructions, make sure you include them on the page (and keep them updated).

Include a **Change log** section which lists changes in the plugin through the versions.

After you publish a new version, it would probably be a good idea to write a blog post about it and add a comment with version changes to the comments on the plugin page.

Insights

Insights brings a powerful new way to write your blog posts. It increases productivity and at the same time the appeal of your posts.

With Insights you can very quickly (in couple of seconds) do the following:

- Search your blog for posts, edit them or insert links to them into the current post
- Insert Flickr Images
- Insert Youtube videos
- Search and link to Wikipedia
- Search Google
- Insert a Google Map

Insights allows you to do all this using dynamic AJAX interface which loads the relevant information to your post in just a few seconds.

Download

- Download: Insights

Using Insights

Insights increases the **speed** you access and present information on your site. It makes any information almost instantaneously available.

Let's say I want to link snazzy archives to my exact plugin page.

If I am not sure of the exact link to that page I would need around 1 minute to open a new window, search for this page, copy the link and paste it. With Insights everything is done in couple of seconds.

Providing support

Thanks to the huge WordPress user base, your plugin will typically be downloaded at least a few hundred or or perhaps even thousands of times. If your plugin gets popular, you can expect tens of thousands or even hundreds of thousands of downloads.

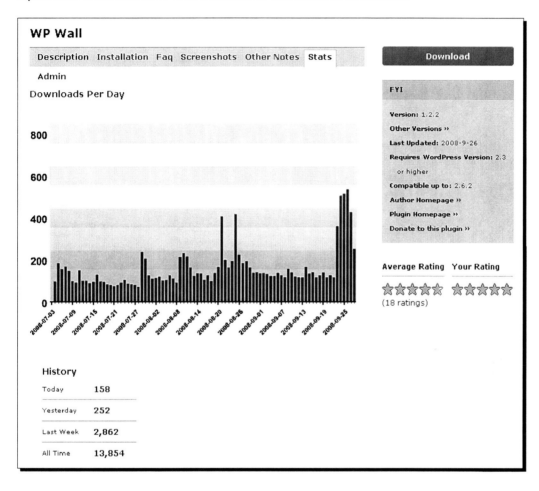

When you have thousands of people downloading the plugin, be prepared to have hundreds coming to your site and asking questions.

Most users will first look for answers in the `readme.txt` file or your plugin page, before they send a direct question. So, it is important to have these files prepared well.

Useful support tips

Make sure you create good documentation. This small investment in time will return itself many times over in the long run.

When you answer a particular support question, consider adding it to the FAQ part of the `readme.txt` file if you think that can help other users as well.

Try to engage users to help each other out. Users have a tendency to discover things by themselves, and they love to share it - make sure you encourage it. This will save your own time later.

If a user reports an error in the plugin, try to fix it and update the plugin as soon as possible, especially if it is a security related problem.

No matter how hard you try, there will always be users who have never read your readme file or the plugin page and have come straight with a question. Don't get mad at them.

If the plugin becomes very popular and the comment system is not enough to cover all issues, you may consider opening a support forum. There are several forum plugins for WordPress (bbPress, SimplePress, and so on) and also stand alone solutions (SMF, Vanilla, and so on.) that can be integrated with WordPress.

Code management and plugin repository

WordPress provides a free home for any plugin at the WordPress Plugin Directory, found at `http://wordpress.org/extend/plugins/`. It simply represents a frontend to the WordPress SVN repository found at `wp-plugins.org`.

Subversion (also known as SVN) is software that allows you to easily store and manage your plugin projects (you can find a SVN FAQ at `http://subversion.tigris.org/faq.html`).

Once in the WordPress SVN, everyone will be able to **check out** (download) a copy of your plugin, but only you, as a plugin author, will have the ability to **commit** changes to the plugin in the repository.

Requesting repository access

In order to gain write access to the repository, you need to fill out the Request form found at `http://wordpress.org/extend/plugins/add/`.

You will need to provide:

1. A plugin name
2. A short description
3. An URL to the plugin homepage

WordPress Plugins » Requests
Add Your Plugin

I want WordPress to host the plugin I wrote. **How will this work?**

You can add the plugin **you've written** to the plugin directory by filling out the form below. This will give you access to a **subversion repository** where you can put your plugin.

This form is only for **plugin developers**. If you'd like to see a plugin listed here, please contact that plugin's author.

Plugin Name (required)

Post Types

Plugin Description (required)

    Provides pre-defined post templates to quickly add a photo or a link to your blog.

Plugin URL

v.prelovac.com/vladimir/wordpress-plugins/post-types

Send Post »

The access will usually be granted in a couple of days, and the best way to use the time while you wait is to polish your `readme.txt` file. Prepare the screenshots, and tweak the plugin page.

Using SVN

Once your request has been approved, you will get an email with the details for accessing your repository. For example, it may be: `http://svn.wp-plugins.org/wp-wall`.

To access it, you need to use SVN. There are various SVN frontends, but no matter which one you use, the procedure for setting up your plugin for the first time is the same. The following example uses the TortoiseSVN client for Windows (`http://tortoisesvn.tigris.org`).

Time for action - Manage a local repository using SVN

1. Create a directory where your local copy of the plugin will be stored, for example, `D:\plugins\wp-wall`.

2. Then perform the action—checkout from the repository (right-click the folder and select the **SVN Checkout**). You need to type in the URL that you received when repository access was granted for your plugin.

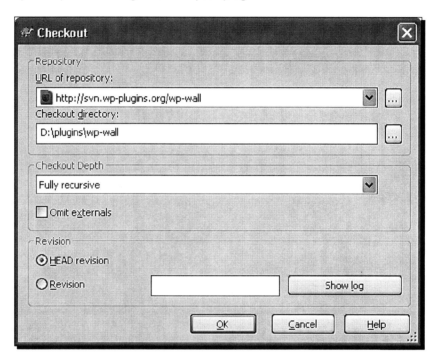

3. When you perform a checkout, you will have three empty folders: `trunk`, `branches`, and `tags`. Copy your plugin files to the trunk folder (for example, you now have `trunk/wp-wall.php`).

4. Create a new folder in `tags`, for example, `0.1` (your initial plugin version), and copy the plugin files there as well.

5. Commit the changes to the repository (for example, right-click and select **SVN Commit...**).

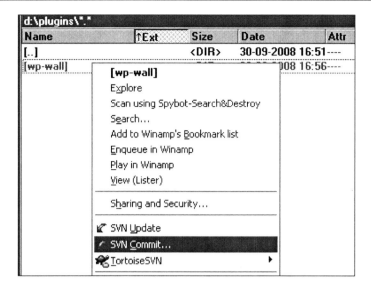

What just happened?

First, we created a local copy of the repository using **SVN checkout**. This copies the necessary file structure to your disk. Note that you can also use SVN checkout later, if for example, you lost the files, or you want to update a plugin from a different computer.

Next, we moved our plugin files to the trunk folder. When you download a plugin from WordPress.org, you will get the archived contents of the trunk folder. We have also copied our files to the `0.1` folder in the tags folder (we have 'tagged' our versions). This allows us to revert to a previous version at a later time.

Finally, we **commited** our plugin to the repository, and soon, it will be publically available for download at `www.WordPress.org`!

Tagging a new version

When you create a new version of the plugin, the process is similar.

1. Make sure you changed the version number in your main PHP file.

2. Create a new folder under `tags`, for example `0.2`, and copy your plugin files from the `trunk` folder. If you are on Windows, every folder under `trunk/` will have `.svn` folders. You should not copy them.

3. Commit the changes for all the files.

Using WordPress development SVN

WordPress core is developed using SVN. This means that you can also at anytime checkout the latest development version. This allows you to see what is going on under the hood, for example, to test your plugins before a new version of WordPress is officially released.

The fastest way to do this is to have a development version of WordPress running on your local computer. On Linux and Mac OS, this should not be a big problem, and Windows users can use packages such as EasyPHP (http://www.easyphp.org) to set up the PHP/MySQL development environment.

You can even have a development version on a shared web hosting account, as many web hosting companies allow **SSH(Secure Shell)** or **jailed SSH** access to your account (you may want to inquire with your hosting provider about this).

Once you have a Unix-like shell available, you can check out the latest Wordpress build using the following commands:

```
$ mkdir devwp
$ cd devwp
$ svn co http://svn.automattic.com/wordpress/trunk/ .
```

To check out a specific version, you would use:

```
$ svn co http://svn.automattic.com/wordpress/tags/2.5.1.
```

 Web based SVN packages such as PHPSVNClient (http://code.google.com/p/phpsvnclient/) could allow you to check out the latest version of WordPress to your site, even if you do not have shell access to your server.

Local copy of plugin repository

Just like you can check out WordPress core, you are also free to check out the entire WordPress plugin repository.

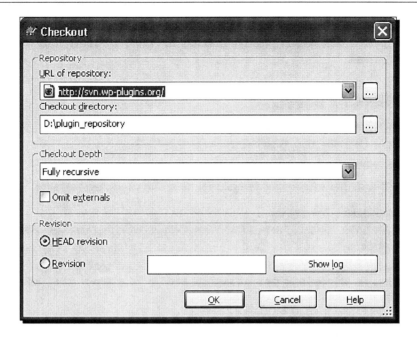

Be warned that this may take quite a while.

The advantage of having a local copy of the plugin repository is to easily search through all plugins when you need a reference to a function or an idea on how to create certain functionalities.

Quick reference

WordPress Plugin Directory: `http://wordpress.org/extend/plugins`

Request repository access: `http://wordpress.org/extend/plugins/add`

Updating WordPress with SVN: `http://codex.wordpress.org/Installing/Updating_WordPress_with_Subversion`

SVN help and tool downloads: `http://subversion.tigris.org`

Easy PHP: `http://www.easyphp.org`

PHPSVN Client: `http://code.google.com/p/phpsvnclient/`

SVN help and tool downloads: `http://subversion.tigris.org`

Promotion

After your plugin is finished and the documentation is ready, it's time to announce your new plugin to the world.

We have already covered how to host the plugin in the WordPress Plugin Directory, which is the most important first step in plugin promotion. But there are some other interesting places to visit as well.

Plugin promotion checklist

1. Head to the WordPress Plugins and Hacks forums (`http://wordpress.org/support/forum/10`).

2. Create a new topic, for example, [New plugin: Insights].

3. Use a simple but informative template to describe your plugin release.

   ```
   Plugin Name: Insights
   Plugin URL: http://www.prelovac.com/vladimir/wordpress-plugins/
   insights

   Description: Insights brings a powerful new way to write your blog
   posts. It increases productivity and at the same time the appeal
   of your posts.
   ```

4. Visit the Weblog Tools Collection forum (`http://weblogtoolscollection.com/news/forum/new-wordpress-plugins`) and create a topic there as well, using the same template. After guys from the Weblog Tools Collection site review the topic, it should be added to their regular plugin news post, which appears on the dashboard of every WordPress user.

5. Add your plugin to `http://wp-plugins.net`. This is another place where users will look for a plugin.

6. Add your plugin to the WordPress Plugin Compatibility list (`http://codex.wordpress.org/Plugins/Plugin_Compatibility`). You need to register before you can add changes to the list.

7. Announce the plugin on your blog.

These steps will almost guarantee that you get enough downloads, feedbacks, reviews, and support questions.

General plugin development guidelines

WordPress does not enforce any strict rules on plugins, and plugins have complete control over the WordPress web site. It is important to understand this and underline security and performance implications if plugins do not follow general **good behaviour** guidelines.

Security

Exploits such as SQL injection or **Cross-Site Request Forgery** (**CSRF**) may pose serious security threat to the users of your plugin, if particular care is not taken.

WordPress provides simple mechanisms to prevent these threats.

- ◆ `$wpdb->prepare()`, `$wpdb->insert()`, `$wpdb->update()`: These are database functions that should be used for creating database queries and inserting/updating the information.
- ◆ `wp_nonce_url()`: This function is used for links, and `wp_nonce_field()` is a function used for forms in combination with `check_admin_referer()`/`check_ajax_referer()` that will protect your requests against CSRF.

Performance

If you not careful, plugins can sometimes create serious overhead issues and affect the performance of the entire site. Therefore, it is important to follow general performance guidelines and these tips:

- ◆ Take care of the number of your MySQL queries. If you need to use several complicated queries, you can use built-in WordPress cache (which we covered in Chapter 4).

  To enable caching, add this line to the WordPress `wp-config.php` file:

  ```
  define('WP_CACHE', true);
  ```

- ◆ Loading plugin localization data only when necessary (as shown in Chapter 7) is another performance improvement.
- ◆ The same goes for JavaScript usage—load the scripts only on those pages where your plugin needs them.
- ◆ In Chapter 7, we also covered how to hook to actions and filters only on those pages where your plugin needs them. That way, we do not add a burden to the WordPress engine when they are not needed.
- ◆ Generally optimization means to use only those resources that are required to do the job.

Re-using resources

The best WordPress plugins will try to make the most most of the functions provided by WordPress.

By using WordPress functions for handling uploaded files, storing posts or displaying information, you are making sure your code works properly in all the future WordPress versions. The best thing about all this is that you will get a **free ride** on all future upgrades to that functionality.

An example of this is the way we used WordPress comment system to handle shouts on the wall for the WP Wall plugin.

In case you need to save simple data in the database, you can re-use the WordPress options table which is capable of storing almost any kind of information.

Keeping API up-to-date

- WordPress is still in rapid development, and API functions change with each new version.

- Make sure you always use the latest API functions.

- To help you find any deprecated functions and include the files that you may have used, WordPress provides two action hooks:

```
deprecated_function_run($oldfunction, $newfunction)
deprecated_file_included($oldfile, $newfile)
```

- In order to use them, you need to set the WP_DEBUG global variable in `wp-config.php`:

```
define('WP_DEBUG', true);
```

These two hooks will allow you to discover deprecated code and make your plugin much more resilient to future WordPress upgrades.

Quick reference

wpdb class: `http://codex.wordpress.org/Function_Reference/wpdb_Class`

Deprecated function hooks: `http://codex.wordpress.org/WordPress_Deprecated_Functions_Hook`

WordPress cache: `http://codex.wordpress.org/Function_Reference/WP_Cache`

SQL injection: `http://en.wikipedia.org/wiki/Sql_injection`

Cross-site request forgery: `http://en.wikipedia.org/wiki/Cross-site_request_forgery`

WordPress MU development

WordPress MU is a multi-user, multi-blog version of WordPress and it is quickly gaining popularity. It allows you to run many blogs from a single installation of the WordPress MU software.

The WordPress MU homepage is located at `http://mu.wordpress.org`, and from here, you can access the latest version.

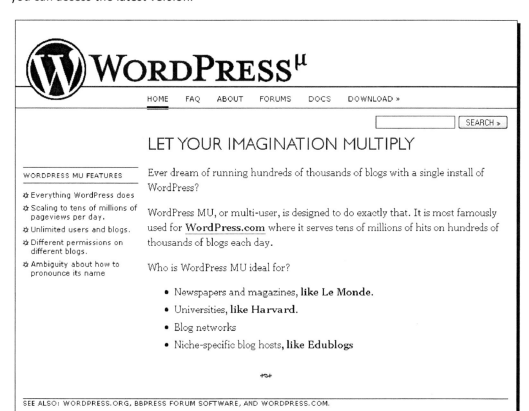

Although, WordPress MU re-uses 90% of the WordPress code, there are some differences between the two, mainly due to the fact that MU is meant to host multiple blogs simultaneously.

For example, if you were creating an XML sitemap plugin for normal WordPress, and created the file by default in the root of the blog, it would not work on MU, as each blog would be overwriting the sitemap every time it was generated.

Other differences come from the fact that WordPress MU is not always updated at the same time with WordPress. So if you use new features and API functions available in the latest version of WordPress, they may not work in the latest version of WordPress MU; that's something to keep your eye on.

Finally, WordPress MU supports additional API functions and global variables mainly used to support the multiple blog MU environment. Find more about them at this address: `http://codex.wordpress.org/WPMU_Functions`

If you want to make sure your plugin is compatible with WordPress MU, the best thing to do is to have a local version of MU installed as a testing ground.

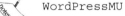

Quick reference

WordPress MU: `http://mu.wordpress.org`

Codex for WordPress MU: `http://codex.wordpress.org/WordPressMU`

Exclusive WPMU functions: `http://codex.wordpress.org/WPMU_Functions`

Exclusive WPMU variables: `http://codex.wordpress.org/WPMU_Global_Variables`

WordPress and GPL

WordPress is licensed under GNU **General Public License** (**GPL**), which has several implications to your plugins.

The most important one is that plugin code using WordPress functions automatically becomes GPL as well. This still means you can sell your plugins. But it also means that anyone who buys it or downloads it from the Internet is free to modify it and even resell it without asking for your permission.

A commercially oriented approach to plugin development is still possible, as most clients will be interested in a long-term relationship, with support and plugin updates included.

Technically speaking, there might be a way to license your code differently if you created it in the following way:

1. Write most of your code as a library, without any WordPress calls.
2. Create a WordPress plugin that will call the functions from your library.

This way, only the WordPress plugin becomes GPL, and you can license the library separately.

The GPL license is still subject to many different interpretations, even by its creators; so make sure you consult the latest GPL FAQ (`http://www.gnu.org/licenses/gpl-faq.html`) for all your questions.

Online resources

The following online resources can be the starting point for expanding your knowledge on WordPress development.

WordPress documentation (WordPress Codex)

The WordPress Codex is a huge library of information to which anyone can contribute. It contains API information, **how to?** guides, tutorials, and much more.

```
http://codex.wordpress.org/Main_Page
```

WordPress development news

To get information regarding the latest development news, we can visit the following web sites:

WordPress blog

The official blog for WordPress is `www.wordpress.org`. It publishes the latest news regarding the new versions and other current WordPress.org activities.

```
http://wordpress.org/development/
```

WordPress development updates

This site has the latest news on WordPress core development, straight from the developers.

```
http://wpdevel.wordpress.com/
```

WordPress Trac

If you need more in-depth information about what is going on with WordPress, you can take a peek at WordPress Trac. All reported bugs and new feature requests are listed here.

```
http://trac.wordpress.org/
```

WordPress dev IRC channel

Meet all the developers, and chat about the hottest development topics in this IRC Channel.

```
irc.freenode.net, channel #wordpress-dev
```

Debugging and testing

The following debugging and testing methods can be carried out to debug and test the code:

Unit testing

Unit testing allows you to set up independent tests for individual blocks of code and control, to determine if they function properly under various circumstances.

```
http://simpletest.org/
```

```
http://www.phpunit.de/
```

Automated tests

This website provides extensive testing and fine-tuning capabilities for all aspects of WordPress execution.

```
http://codex.wordpress.org/Automated_Testing
```

Mailing Lists

A mailing list is a forum for discussing all the issues related to WordPress. The following are some examples of the mailing lists.

WP hackers

This is a mailing list for the discussion of latest development trends in WordPress, advanced plugin ideas and other serious matters:

```
http://lists.automattic.com/mailman/listinfo/wp-hackers
```

WP professionals

There is always a need for good WordPress professionals, and this is the list where they are found. Make sure you are subscribed here, if you are looking for work.

```
http://lists.automattic.com/mailman/listinfo/wp-pro
```

Other mailing lists

There are many other mailing lists of interest such as lists focused on documentation, testing, support, and so on.

```
http://codex.wordpress.org/Mailing_Lists
```

Podcasts

These are podcasts I enjoy listening to, related to WordPress development and general news. You can often find WordPress developers logged-in as guests, discussing new plugins and techniques.

WordCast

WordCast is an open source project, which enables people to know what their friends are thinking & doing via an Internet browser or desktop application.

```
http://wordcastpodcast.com/
```

WordPress Weekly

WordPress Weekly was a weekly podcast that discussed what happened in the world of WordPress during the week. Generally, every show was an open round table discussion. The show is no longer running, but old episodes are still available.

```
http://www.wptavern.com/wordpress-weekly
```

Author's (Vladimir Prelovac's) web site

This is my home page, and source of WordPress related information.

```
http://www.prelovac.com/vladimir
```

Summary

In this chapter, we have learned about:

- Plugin localization
- Publishing and maintaining WordPress plugins
- Using SVN repository
- GPL licensing model
- WordPress MU differences
- Online WordPress development resources

Obviously, a combination of flexibility and a great user base make WordPress the most appealing Internet development platform today. In addition, WordPress experts are among the most wanted Internet professionals.

From the first chapter to this last, we learned how to develop WordPress plugins in a modern development environment. I hope you can put this knowledge to good use and express your creativity by using WordPress.

Index

insights 15
is_admin() 62
is_page() 50
is_single() 50

J

JavaScript
  and WordPress 67
  parameters parsing, wp_localize_script used 79
  using, with WordPress 79
jQuery
  CSS, applying to pop-up 70
  document, modifying 69
  examples 68
  initializing 68
  JavaScript and WordPress 67
  mouse hover event, implementing 63-67
  pop-up creating, CSS used 70
  web site 69
  web site, for examples 69
jQuery.Ajax method
  about 81
  advanced Ajax call, using 81, 82
jQuery JavaScript library. *See* **jQuery**
js_escape() 50

L

link, posting quickly
  link template, adding 224-228
Live Blogroll plugin 13
localization
  about 202
  plugin, creating 203-206
  support, adding 203-206
  usage, optimizing 206, 207
  working 207
localization files, creating
  new translation, creating 248, 249
  POT file, updating 247
  POT file creating, Poedit used 244-246
  translation, updating 249

M

mailing lists, online resources
  other mailing lists 270

WP hackers 270
WP professionals 270
manage panel, programming
  existing column, modifying 233, 234
  post type column, adding 231-233
  screen search filter, managing 234
  search filter box, adding 235, 236

N

nonce
  about 82
  security nonce, adding 83

O

online resources
  about 269
  Authors (Vladimir Prelovacs) web site 271
  automated tests 270
  code, debugging 270
  code, testing 270
  mailing lists 270
  podcasts 271
  unit testing 270
  WordPress development news 269
  WordPress documentation (WordPress Codex)
    269

P

plugin
  blogroll, starting up 57-62
  creating 28-30
  describing, PHP class used 126-129
  Digg link, displaying 32-35
  hooks 39
  plugin information header, adding 30
  used, in book 12
  version check, testing 31, 32
  WordPress version, checking 30, 31
plugin, installing
  documentation, searching 23, 25
  steps 22, 23
plugin, managing 23
plugin class
  creating 126-129
  creating, PHP class used 126, 128, 129

Thank you for buying
WordPress Plugin Development Beginner's Guide

Packt Open Source Project Royalties

When we sell a book written on an Open Source project, we pay a royalty directly to that project. Therefore by purchasing WordPress Plugin Development Beginner's Guide, Packt will have given some of the money received to the WordPress project.

In the long term, we see ourselves and you—customers and readers of our books—as part of the Open Source ecosystem, providing sustainable revenue for the projects we publish on. Our aim at Packt is to establish publishing royalties as an essential part of the service and support a business model that sustains Open Source.

If you're working with an Open Source project that you would like us to publish on, and subsequently pay royalties to, please get in touch with us.

Writing for Packt

We welcome all inquiries from people who are interested in authoring. Book proposals should be sent to author@packtpub.com. If your book idea is still at an early stage and you would like to discuss it first before writing a formal book proposal, contact us; one of our commissioning editors will get in touch with you.

We're not just looking for published authors; if you have strong technical skills but no writing experience, our experienced editors can help you develop a writing career, or simply get some additional reward for your expertise.

About Packt Publishing

Packt, pronounced 'packed', published its first book "Mastering phpMyAdmin for Effective MySQL Management" in April 2004 and subsequently continued to specialize in publishing highly focused books on specific technologies and solutions.

Our books and publications share the experiences of your fellow IT professionals in adapting and customizing today's systems, applications, and frameworks. Our solution-based books give you the knowledge and power to customize the software and technologies you're using to get the job done. Packt books are more specific and less general than the IT books you have seen in the past. Our unique business model allows us to bring you more focused information, giving you more of what you need to know, and less of what you don't.

Packt is a modern, yet unique publishing company, which focuses on producing quality, cutting-edge books for communities of developers, administrators, and newbies alike. For more information, please visit our website: www.PacktPub.com.

PUBLISHING

WordPress for Business Bloggers

Promote and grow your WordPress blog with advanced plugins, analytics, advertising, and SEO

Paul Thewlis

PACKT

WordPress for Business Bloggers

ISBN: 978-1-847195-32-6   Paperback: 327 pages

Promote and grow your WordPress blog with advanced plug-ins, analytics, advertising, and SEO

1. Gain a competitive advantage with a well polished WordPress business blog

2. Develop and transform your blog with strategic goals

3. Create your own custom design using the Sandbox theme

4. Apply SEO (search engine optimization) to your blog

3. Market and measure the success of your blog

WordPress
Theme Design

A complete guide to creating professional WordPress themes

Tessa Blakeley Silver

PACKT

WordPress Theme Design

ISBN: 978-1-847193-09-4   Paperback: 211 pages

A complete guide to creating professional WordPress themes

1. Take control of the look and feel of your WordPress site

2. Simple, clear tutorial to creating Unique and Beautiful themes

3. Expert guidance with practical step-by-step instructions for theme design

4. Design tips, tricks, and troubleshooting ideas

Please check **www.PacktPub.com** for information on our titles

Learning Drupal 6 Module Development

ISBN: 978-1-847194-44-2   Paperback: 310 pages

A practical tutorial for creating your first Drupal 6 modules with PHP

1. Specifically written for Drupal 6 development

2. Program your own Drupal modules

3. No experience of Drupal development required

4. Know Drupal 5? Learn what's new in Drupal 6

5. Integrate AJAX functionality with the jQuery library

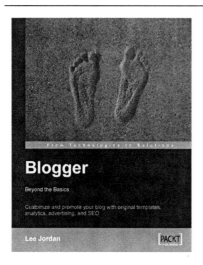

Blogger: Beyond the Basics

ISBN: 978-1-847193-17-9   Paperback: 380 pages

Customize and promote your blog with original templates, analytics, advertising, and SEO

1. Customize your Blogger templates

2. Grow your blog into a professional, feature-rich site

3. Add social bookmarks to your blog

4. Optimize your blog with SEO

5. Integrate analytics and advertising with your Blogger blog

6. Concise, clear, and easy to follow; rich with examples

Please check **www.PacktPub.com** for information on our titles

Printed in the United Kingdom by
Lightning Source UK Ltd., Milton Keynes
142422UK00001B/71/P